Dedication

I dedicate this book to me mam and dad, Defiance and Lenard Smith, who were my fantastic Romani parents.

Me mam and dad at a scramble in Frome in the '50s

Maggie Smith-Bendell BEM

Old Days And Old Ways

AUSTIN MACAULEY PUBLISHERS™
LONDON · CAMBRIDGE · NEW YORK · SHARJAH

Copyright © Maggie Smith-Bendell BEM (2018)

The right of Maggie Smith-Bendell BEM to be identified as author of this work has been asserted by her in accordance with section 77 and 78 of the Copyright, Designs and Patents Act 1988.
F
All rights reserved. No part of this publication may be reproduced, stored in a retrieval system, or transmitted in any form or by any means, electronic, mechanical, photocopying, recording, or otherwise, without the prior permission of the publishers.

Any person who commits any unauthorised act in relation to this publication may be liable to criminal prosecution and civil claims for damages.

A CIP catalogue record for this title is available from the British Library.

ISBN 9781788486989 (Paperback)
ISBN 9781788486996 (Hardback)
ISBN 9781788487009 (E-Book)

www.austinmacauley.com

First Published (2018)
Austin Macauley Publishers Ltd™
25 Canada Square
Canary Wharf
London
E14 5LQ

Our gypsy history is dark and sometimes very sad due to misunderstanding, prejudice and suspicion of our race.

Chapter 1
15 July 1941

On this fine, hot, sunny July day, a new-born baby girl—the size of a skinned rabbit—was born on the edge of a pea field deep in the heart of Somerset. Yes, that baby was yours truly, Margaret Smith, who became known as Maggie Smith-Bendell in her later years. They say my first cries could be heard right across the many rows of peas awaiting to be picked—after a smarting slap on my skinny bottom to kick-start me up to my gypsy lifestyle. And what a great, fulfilling life I was born and reared to have!

My parents were the well-known Somerset, Smith/Butler and the Smalls/Blacks of Devonshire. I was lucky enough to be born to two of the oldest Romani gypsy families from these areas—for which I've always been grateful because our way of life gave me a very rich in happiness kind of life—as it did to my seven brothers and sisters. As children, we saw and felt untold love and security from my mum, Defiance Small, and my dad, Lenard Smith, and from extended family on both sides, except just one person, who came very close to hating my mum and dads' little chicks (as he called us). That one fly in the ointment was my dad's old mum, Emma Smith, who was a spiteful nasty old woman, but more of that old darling later.

For ten days, my mum had to lay in the wagon when I was born—this was the way things were done back then—with the district nurse, fresh off her bike ride, checking out mother and baby each day. The visits would smell of Dettol; every crook and corner of the wagon was wiped down with this smelly Dettol just before the nurse was due to call—why I really don't know—because our wagon was kept spotless as were our bodies, clothes and bedding. It must have been the wood smoke lingering in our thick hair, from the outside fire, but it kept the old nurse happy smelling the stinky stuff. After ten days, the nurse allowed my mum out the wagon but would still call a few times in and out to check all was well.

I was born in 1941, the beginning of the Second World War, so I can't remember much about it. As I got older and sat by our yog (fire) listening to the many tales of life during and right after the war years, I learned a great deal. Many hours we would spend sitting cross-legged around the yog—giving way to the person telling or repeating an old tale, so that we could hear every word and log it in our memories, of which we were very good at doing. Some of the tales told were many generations old, but were still being repeated, much like the settled community would read an old book belonging to their family.

While theirs was written in words on paper, our tales were not, because very few, if any Romanies, could write or read—they could only make a mark, which was a 'cross' and witnessed by whoever needed that mark, made most likely in courts when fines had to be paid for lighting fires on the grass verge of the highway, or hawking without a license. These fines were quite common, my dad was fined for being drunk in charge of a horse and cart, and I think my dear old granddad, Dannal, was fined for being blind drunk on a push bike, with a horse tied to the bike saddle. He had, so the tale goes, rode the horse to the pub when he was drunk. As a hand cart, he purchased a push bike from some mush in the pub—in his old befuddled beer soaked head—he worked out how to get the horse and bike back to the stopping place. He would ride the bike and tie his horse on the back of it, but the horse had other ideas. It had been tied up outside that pub long enough, and it wanted to get back to its pals by the wagons. So, it took off in that direction, dragging granddad and his bike with it; hence the gaver (police) who was standing nearby- arrested granddad. He was fined seven shillings and six pence in the magistrate court for being drunk in charge of both horse and bike. He escaped being fined for making a public nuisance. If you did a crime back then, you surely paid the fine or went to jail for one calendar month.

We only had one real human enemy back in those days and that was the police, or gavers as we knew them to be in our Romani language, who most loved, tormenting our families and moving them out of their area—yet a few would turn a blind eye, knowing after a few days we would shift out of our own accord to a new stopping place a few miles up the road. Of course there were stopping places where we could stay to our heart's content—while working on the land or pulled in on to a Common and there were many such commons stretching all over the country. Common land used by all, even to graze sheep and cattle; it was a free place to stop if needed by my community and many others.

Times were harder for the house dweller than us lot after the war. I think the people living in towns found it harder than the folks in the outlying villages of the country side—these families all had gardens to grow vegetables, and the farms to supply the butcher shops with fresh meat, milk, butter, cheese and sometimes cream. Also most farms grew swedes, cabbages and spuds—then there was the bean and pea fields—because we worked on such farms we fared better than most for food, and also we could supply the shops with fresh caught rabbits, pheasants or wild ducks. Our problem was the majority of house dwellers never had the money to spend with us to buy our pegs or flowers, so some days after the end of the war, things got very tight and we were looking for paid work most weeks. It was a slow recovery from a long old war if we didn't work and earn. We couldn't spend money on buying rags or scrap savings, which had dwindled away supplementing bad days. Everyone had to live, and we had the will to live and make sure the young had a chance to grow up fit and healthy. When I say we, I mean all the parents and grandparents. Every one of the families played their parts in our lifestyle or way of living to bring us back on track for, like the settled community, we too lost many of our men-folk to the war. We too had young widows, or mothers with no sons or husbands, to help them recover a long life's long road.

We all lived on the ration books, but the life we led brought us to many farms where we could save coupons by working for meat or vegetables, plus a few bob jingling in our pockets—that's if we got lucky. The old saying goes 'the Gypsy man can make his own luck'—I can't say that is true, it seemed hard work made them their luck; what luck they had they worked many hours a day for, in all winds and weather, as did the women-folk in the family.

Lots of things were scarce such as iron; if we came across a blacksmith who had horse shoe iron in plenty, our men would have several pairs of shoes made for their horses, which would be packed safely away for times of need at least they got new shoes, the rest of us never knew the meaning of owning something brand new. Our clothes and shoes were begged or battered off of some of the house dwellers and right glad of them we were back then.

It took several years for our lives to get remotely back to what it was before the war. We just loved and had to keep travelling seeking work from the view of on lookers. Our lives were very simple ones indeed back then, but there was a little more to it than that. Unlike today, we had no electricity or running water so when it came to thinking of stopping places, we had to think of water, spring water. My lot knew of most of the layout routes of the springs in their area so if possible, we would head to where these springs sprang out from the ground to get good, clean and healthy fresh water, which we did most of the time, but if it was not possible, we would knock on a house dwellers' door for cans of water. The thing was, we did not like pipe water, as my lot called it, as it never had that spring taste to it; but beggars can't be choosers and we were glad of the home owners' kindness in filling up our water cans.

Then, there was the skill of making the old outside fire—you would naturally think it was a case of chucking a heap of wood on the ground and setting light to it, but that was not so. This is because we used heavy thick iron pots-pans and kettles—the fire was built to be able, in the fastest time possible, to bring these things to the boil by just chucking a heap of wood on the ground and setting fire to it. This meant it could take hours to boil a kettle.

But our men had the knack or skill, if you like to build and make a fire that would in a short time have the old kettle singing happily away. The yogs, as we called them, were built with a great deal of care, with a full middle part that could be constantly fed with thin pieces of wood to build up the heat needed for cooking and tea—living the way we did back then, everything had to be thought about, even to the kind of hedges we used to hang our washing on. We liked thick blackthorn hedges, which the washing could be hung on to the thorns, so as not to drop off.

Washing was a right hard job in those days as galvanised buckets were used to boil up the water, which most likely was taken from a spring or stream or fast-flowing brooks. Once boiled, it was poured into the washing tub. The tub was again made of galvanise, in the meantime a fresh bucket was put over the yog to boil up the white washing—such as pudding clothes, tea towels, table cloths and bedding and a separate bucket would be boiling up the towelling nappies. Our women took high pride in their washing, all stains had to be scrubbed or boiled out before they were hung on the hedge. It would be a shame-faced woman who never kept her whites white, and the other women would be only be too quick to tell her so, because she would not only be letting her self down but the others along with her. Thus, dirty washing was not to be tolerated—it got us a bad name, by who ever saw it.

We had no ovens to bake our food in, but the big black iron pots could be used to do a roast in. These pots and pans was scoured inside-out after each meal. It was not any easy task because they were big and heavy, and would get very sooty from the fire. A lot of salt and soda was used to keep them fresh and clean. The women, if they had any, would rub bacon rine on the pots and pans to stop them from rusting. When not in use, iron doesn't take long to get rusty. So, this was another job that was done by the women looking after their pot ware.

They say a woman's work is never done— that's quite right because on top of cooking, washing and looking after their children, the wagons had to be cleaned, waxed and polished. They had to do all these jobs after a long day hawking around the outlying villages. On warm sunny days, all the bedding would be hung out to air, picked off the hedge and finally shook out to get rid of insects, and placed back on the beds.

To be able to sit around the yog with their men-folk on an evening was pure bliss for the Romani women—cleaning finished—children washed and put to bed. It was now their time for relaxing and chatting so it proves life was not all travelling and pleasure for the Romani women—just adding to that—even in their relaxing time, they could still be making crepe paper roses or bunching up dozens of bunches of wild flowers for hawking out the next morning. But they could be at peace sitting round the old yog with their men when doing these little jobs while the men made the wooden clothes pegs or wooden headed flowers. These couples never had much time to spare or to themselves as there was always things that just had to be done.

As for the men of the family, their lives was just as full—wagons had to be maintained, checks had to be made on the condition of their wagon homes on wheels, repairs needed were carried out, and then their beloved faithful horses had to be cared for. Our lives depended greatly on these animals.

In fact, they were the very core or centre of our day today living. So much were they relied on to get us from place to place that they were looked after better than most humans. A Romani man can spot in a second if his grey (horse) is in some sort of pain or trouble. He will stand with head to one side as I've so often witnessed looking the horse over from head to tail, spotting the problem. Most of the horse problems our men can cure or sort out themselves, they very rarely call on the vet. The understanding between horse and owner takes some beating within my community, to make sure his horse is kept fit and healthy, only the best grass or grazing that can be had will do. Even to the point of 'pooving their grey' which means slipping it in the farmer's best grass field after dark and removing it at peep of day light or spending hours cutting the grass herby banks and feeding it to their horses. Because of our life style, our horses spend most of the time when we have pulled off the road for a few days on plug chains—for their own safety to stop them from wandering away and getting knocked down by the traffic.

In winter, I've known the men to take on awful hard farm work just to provide that much needed few bales of hay. Such jobs as swede topping in the hard frost or being hidden under a heavy snow fall which has frozen the swedes into the ground. This was, I believe, one of the most unwelcome winter jobs, but at times needs must come first. Because of the harsh, wintery, cold weather working on the swede fields, it brought terrible accidents—the long sharp knives used to top the swedes could slip out of cold hands and cut a leg to the bone or cut off fingers. Sometimes the men working in pairs would light a fire to have a warm-by but if the farmer thought they was wasting too much time he would kick the fire out and give them a verbal warning. He was docking some of their pay, then an almighty row would break out between my dad and the farmer mush. Uncle Jim, my dad's brother, whom we travelled with a great deal came back to our wagons hopping mad at me dad one cold winter morning. I believe we were working on a farm up in Wiltshire, and Uncle Jim and my dad had got this swede topping job on a local farm. Having been out since first light, working like slaves kicking the swedes out the ground ready to top them. My dad and Jim got very cold, so my dad gathered up some wood and lit his yog to thaw out by. They were scrammed and stiff with the cold—but from the farm yard the farmer had spotted the rising smoke and took off after his two lazy workers as he thought of them. So hollering at the top of his lungs at my dad as he stood getting warm by his now blazing yog, the farmer tore into my dad, calling him a lazy no-good gypsy bastard—"What am I paying you for? Not to stand by a fire all day."

Open-mouthed both our men watched as the farmer kicked the fire in all directions, sparks and smoke high on choking. Jim and my dad who were so stiff with the cold, they could not move out the way quick enough and took the brunt of the farmer's anger.

If only the farmer had took time to look at what they had done that morning before losing his rage, he would have found that a fair morning's work had been already done. This is because we too needed the pay and hay as they had put their backs in the work. Instead, he shouted that he was paying them to top swedes, not stand round a fire all day. "Lazy good for nothings," he added. These words were so belittling to hardworking gypsy men who would work at any job to earn their living,

"Lazy good for nothing," my dad hollered back, "I'll give you lazy good for nothing, you snotty nosed pup; if you are that worried about your swedes, I'll make you eat 'um." As my dad bent down and picked up a frozen swede, Uncle Jim tried to talk him down.

"No my brother, behave, behave mush."

But by then, my dad had grabbed the mush and was trying to ram a frozen swede down his throat but Jim got between them and broke the fight up. My dad had a bloody nose while the mush had a bloody mouth but all we knew from old that it was not over. We knew the farmer would call in the law.

Jim was very angry with my dad, but it never lasted long. He knew how my dad had felt on reaching our yog. Jim told my mam and his own wife, aunt May, his dinalow (fool) brother had tried to make the farmer mush swallow a frozen swede and they could be in a lot of trouble with the gavers.

Quite some time later, the gavers came with the farmer to our stopping place and asked the farmer to identify his attacker.

The farmer pointed out my dad and then Jim—he was accusing both our men.

Jim was having none of his old buck and told the gavers blow by blow what really did happen, according to Jim that was.

The farmer had run like a lunatic across the field and attacked them both by kicking the fire over him and his brother Lenard—foul mouthing them and calling them names. My dad picked up a swede to throw at the farmer to calm him down. It hit the farmer right in the mouth, quite by accident, mind you, then the farmer punched my dad on the nose.

"God's truth, sir, that's what happened," said Jim.

"And let's hear it from you," they asked my dad.

"It was like this, sir," answered my dad. "We two been out on that swede field since peep of daylight. We had got a good many rows of swedes out and topped, but in the meantime, we both got stiff with the cold so I lit me a fire to warm our hands by. You know only too well sir, this is swede country, and you know about some of the bad accidents caused by frozen hands doing a frozen job. It's happened time and time again over the years. Gods honour, sir, 'tis true."

"So I'll ask you two policemen to walk with us back across that field to not only look at the amount of work we done, but also to see how far this lunatic kicked that fire over us. Would you do that right now, sirs?"

Lo and behold, they both nodded yes that they would look at the evidence of work done and fire damage.

"Dear god," whispered my mum, "I hope my Lenard's telling the truth."

"Don't we all," said May.

"If he wasn't, he could get six months in jail."

And so all five went back to the scene of the crime, and were gone quite a long time.

My mum and aunt May were very worried because the farmer had accused both their men—and if both were sent to jail, it meant we had no men and no kind of help. We would be in a right old mess and all because the men got cold working for an unstable mush. They had been warned by other travellers this farmer could be a queer old bugger to work for. They had had their share of problems with him in the past saying that they never done a fair day's work for a fair day's pay but would my dad listen? No, he knew best, and now he could pay dearly for it alongside my poor innocent uncle Jim.

Aunt May never called my mum 'Little Fiance' as most travellers did because of her size. My mum was known as Little Fiance, not Defiance, her real name. Aunt May called her 'my Vie', the same as my dad did; it was his pet name for her.

"My Vie—what's to become of us lot if they two get put away?"

They had a right to be worried and concerned, because it was very rare indeed that our word would be took as truth before a gorgie's word, when they made accusations against one of ours.

"Well, my May, we made it through the war years without our men half the time, and we never went under then, we shan't now. If the worse comes to the worse, we'll manage somehow, we got to old gal, ain't we eh…"

Then, on sight of the five men coming back to the wagons, both women stood up and awaited to hear the fate of their men.

Me and our Alfie, as worked up and worried as our mum was because we, like the grown-ups, had this deep fear of the gavers, tried to hear every word the gaver mush was now saying to the farmer.

"This is how I shall write my report.

"You, Mr so and so farmer. You interviewed and employed these two Gypsy men to work on your land, for payment in exchange for clearing a field of swedes. Is that correct so far?"

"Yes."

"This being the first day of their work, and you not knowing what time they started to clear the field, noticed smoke from a wood fire and jumped to the conclusion that the two men were not working but wasting their time and yours by standing over a roaring fire. Correct?"

"Yes."

"You then got very angry and ran across the field to the fire and kicked it over the two men. Correct?"

"No."

"You don't agree with their version of what happened, correct?"

"Yes, I mean no."

"What do you mean? Are you now saying that you never kicked the fire over these two men, is that what you're saying?"

"Yes, I never did kick the fire over the men."

"Then could you explain to me, why both men are covered in ashes and holes burnt in their jackets?"

"I can't say how they got like that"

"Can you now that you have taken a long look at the amount of clearing of swedes these two men had carried out before you arrived say it was a fair few hours of work."

"Yes. I'm sorry I did not look to see if they had already done any topping."

At this stage, my dad and Jim's yocks (eyes) were hanging out their heads. This had never happened before, two gavers seeing fair play for two Romani men and against one of their own people. A well-known farmer at that—this would be told and retold till the end of time.

And this is how I know the tale so well, but lost the name of the farmer concerned, because as with some tales the words get changed over time.

"Well Mister, so I'm not going to charge these two with a crime. In my book, it was self-defence, but I'm telling you Gypsies to pack up and move on, and don't come back in to my area. You got lucky today but might not be so lucky next time. Good day!"

It was over. The loss of half a day's work mattered but not being under arrest more than made up for it and they still had the two bales of hay to go on with.

So many of these episodes happened with life on the road. We never knew from day-to-day what kind of trouble, if any, we could walk in to. There are some very strange people out there—and at times we found them or they found us.

This support from the police, for my dad and Jim, was to their knowledge a first in their life time and would be cemented in our fire side tales. It just went to show this farmer mush was well-known to them with his antics against the Romanies who worked for him.

Chapter 2
My Dad's Family

Once more we were back on the road, and said Jim it was time to catch up with and check on the welfare of their parents. I have written quite a lot about my dad's family in my first book, *Our Forgotten Years* but need to bring them in again because we often travelled with all or some of the brothers and sisters.

My dad had quite a big family, whom I shall name so every one of their characters are known. This is because they were indeed characters in their own way, at times even a bit not right in their heads.

But very loyal to each other, and a hard working bunch of people.

Dannal Butler and Emma Smith were my granny and granddad.

Tom, known very fondly as kipper, was the eldest son—married to a beautiful woman called Jane. They had, I believe, four children. Jane died young in her life, and Tom then married Kizzie and had two more children with her.

Jessie married Louie had five and then brought up his sisters baby gal called Tiny after her death in child confinement. Jessie was known as Cripple Jessie.

Joe, known again fondly as cock eyed Joe, married Ally and had two gals.

Lenard and Defiance (my parents) had eight children.

Alfie and Dillion, I believe, had thirteen children.

Jim, married to May, had five children.

John married to Ellen, I believe, had five or maybe six.

Dan married several times and had four with Leal and a second family with Peggy, but I'm not sure how many, it could have been another four.

Emily and Black Smith Joe—this was my aunt who predicted her own death in *Our Forgotten Years*.

Touie married to Henry had two children. Henry was known as squeaker.

When this family fell out—all hollering at each other at the same time, it was like hearing a gaggle of geese bickering—with their deep Somerset accents and my mum's Devonshire one—and the air turned blue with their swearing at each other.

Our families were tight-knit families. We fell in and out, the same as everyone else, but the settled community had a different picture of us in their minds. When we were pulled on a grass verge on a nice day, the women would do their bit of washing and hang it away from the fire out of reach from the smoke on a hedge. People passing by would stop and look at the washing and sometimes shake their heads, but would make no comment to the washers, just give them a backward stare. It was the same when our women were cooking. God knows what they thought we had in them black iron pots, but it seemed to amuse some passers-by. So I thought I would write about our culture and customs and our rules which we live by. Rules that may shock some people, but rules are rules. So I'll write about my own family, how we lived our life and the ups and downs of that life.

The Smith was a huge family when travelling together, twelve wagons and full of small or half-grown children, as well as the grownups, was a sight to be seen. But we were not the biggest family on the road at that time. A lot of families would have up to seventeen grown up children with children of their own. But these families knew very little common illness such as coughs or colds—due to living out in the fresh air. All their lives made us a hardy bunch, with our smoke dried hair and weathered skin, we got on just fine. It was contact with the settled community. We felt that we picked up the whooping cough or measles and diphtheria, all the child illness's that is.

My mum got on quite well with her brothers and sisters-in-law most of the time. Our granddad was a beautiful, kind-hearted old man—not the best looking mush in the world, but had a heart of gold and a temper to run from if you upset him. His love and passion was for his grandchildren, and we all loved and respected him in return.

My old granny was another kettle of fish, but only to my mum and dad and us their children, not to her other sons and daughter's family, just our little family. To say she hated the very sight of my mum would be putting it mildly and only because my mum comes from a different part of the country and my mum's ways never suited the old granny. I think that's how it started out. I once described my old granny to be as sour as a crab apple. She could floor you with a look from her coal black eyes, how I remember those piercing black eyes or yocks, as we know them. She was a big well-built woman always dressed in black with an old trilby to top it off. But there was one thing this old granny could do better than most and that was to cook. Her meals were beautiful and tasty, when cooking broths or stews, whichever son was stopping with her would keep an eye on her. When her meal was nigh on ready to eat, then they would fetch a dish off their women and would go to their mother for a dish of whatever she had cooked. This always happened and was accepted by their wives. Her suety spotted dicks was much sought after. Once cooked and taken out of its muslin clothe to cool down, her family's yocks never left it. She would slice it up into thick slices then spread jam on it. Her sons would scramble to get a piece. All her life she had cooked for ten or twelve at a meal time, so could feed any amount of people. But my old granny had a secret weapon. She and granddad lived in an old hut down the lane and many a time when having a sneaky look from the doorway, I could see lots of old dried up plants hanging from nails, and it was a pinch of these plants she added to her cooking, but never a mention was made of it. I think whatever it was, she took the names of her secret plants to her grave—for I never once heard it discussed after she passed away.

But from my mum, as we got older, we learned of the beatings this old woman caused my mum to get from my dad. In their first few years together—the awful lies the old bitch would tell my dad about my mum brought many a black yock or two, after a hard day's hawking with the old granny and daughters-in-law. Where my mum, with her kind personality, could out-hawk the best of them.

I can now understand the first couple of years my mum putting up with it, after all she was living among a big family. A family with strong family loyalty to each other. My mum being the stranger, the interloper, was made to pay for picking up with my dad. So with no relations of her own, and because she had me and our Alfie, just little ones, she must have suffered a great deal. There was no running back home in them days, you made your bed and had to lay in it.

But enough was enough. Beatings or no beatings, she started to fight back and stand up for herself. Yes it got her in rows and ructions but being named Defiance, she was going to live up to it, not that the old granny let up any. If she couldn't get my dad to back-hander my mum, she would have her spite out on me and our Alfie. God, the names that old woman called us too, and bastard was a mild one. She would try to make us fetch wood and buckets of water all day—give my mum her due, she made sure that we never answered the old granny back. That would never do. I can't say even now, that we never did when out of my mum's ear shot. This is because we picked up some pretty horrible sayings off that old granny and often threw them back at her, when no one else was nearby to hear us.

I know some of my cousins from my dad's family would go blue in the face to read what I write about their old granny Emma but their mothers were fully accepted into the family unit, but my little mother was not. However, now my dear mum and dad have passed on out of this life. I can relate the truth as I know and remember it that bad old granny got my dear mum beat and punched so many times in her early years with my dad that I can neither forgive or forget such violent treatment to a kind-hearted little body like my mum. My granny topped six foot in height, whereas my mum stood less than five foot. In my mum's later years when she lived with me before her passing, she would sit and relate life as it really was back then. The happy, care-free times when they travelled on their own or with Jim and May where they all worked happily, side by side, hawking or pea-picking or out on the hop gardens.

But it was while travelling with the old granny and her daughter Touie that she took the brunt of my dad's beatings. He was young and spiteful back then. It took three children later to make him realise he could lose my mum and his children. She told him enough was enough, that she would set about his old mother and sister, then catch a train back to Devonshire where family would make sure he never found her.

She did indeed set about his sister, although my mum was a small woman. She, on the other hand, was built like a fit pit pony, and could handle herself. But she would never have lifted a hand to the old granny, that would never do. Even though she told my dad she would, she herself would not break the rule. You never lifted your hand to your elders, but she would fight my dad back, or in better words, get her own back. She would wait till he fell asleep and beat him with whatever was near at hand. Mostly the iron swing handled frying pan—with no one brave enough to stick up for her. She had to fight for herself and her children.

There was violence in most of my dad's family marriages and a lot of other families back then. But this was our little mum, my and our Alfie would beg her to take us on the train back to her people. We only knew them as people because we had never met them.

As we sat and chatted about the old days in my day room, I would question her, and she is eighty-five years old by now but her mind as clear as a bell.

"Tell me, Mum, what was the old granny really like?"

"Well, my Maggie, she was as you know a big built old gal. She never really valued your granddad after he became in ill health. I used to feel so sorry for the poor old bugger at times," she told me, with a faraway look in her dear old yocks.

"Why did she pick on you mum?"

"The real reason was, she thought I was a gorgie (non-Romani) and should not be in her family, or with her son. They hated mixed marriages as it thinned their blood line."

"Why did she think you were a gorgie, Mum?"

"Because I had lived a different kind of life to her family and went to school. I could sign my name and to top it all I wore lipstick and powder. She never liked that at all—so set about giving me a dog's life for years. And me and your dad led each other a dog's life because of her. The only time we were really like a family was when we travelled on our own, or with May and Jim, or John and Ellen. That was a lovely time in our lives— no falling out with each other. Your dad was a different man away from his mum and that old Touie."

"You got on well with May and Ellen then," I asked.

"Yes. They were the salt of the earth, them two. Good friends and good company, we would share out everything we begged and what we hawked—they were the best of times. The good times."

"Did the old granny have a go at the other daughter in laws, mum?"

"No. That was one of the things I was quick to notice. In front of me, she would brag um up—how good they were at hawking and keeping their families, and looked after her sons. She always made a fuss and laughed and joked with um in front of me."

"She was a nasty evil old granny mum. Me and our Alfie hated her."

"Hush my Maggie! You should never speak ill of the dead," she said and meant it.

"But Mum, she was nasty to me and our Alfie you know," I answered her.

"I knows she was and so did your dad. And that's why when we were travelling with her or stopped up the Prince lane, we kept you round our yog, as much as we could that is. You two were like two jack rabbits and wanted to play with the other young 'uns, and the old granny used to lay in wait for you two to go round her yog or one close at hand. She would call you nasty names and tell you that you were bastards and a lot of other things, but I always kept a close eye on the both of you."

"Oh I'd hear her and get fightable. I could have ripped her lips off had she been a younger woman."

She now laughed at the thought.

She's a case, my mum. It's good that she can look back and laugh.

"But she was not all that old thinking back, Mum," I laughed.

"No. I think your right there. She just looked old, with her grey hair and smoked dried skin. Did you know, my Maggie, your dad went grey soon after we got together. He had very dark brown hair then when only young, he went as grey as a badger, as did all his brothers and two sisters. It must have been a trait in the family, as they seemed to age in a matter of months, funny that, eh."

"Apart from that, did you find them much different to your own family, Mum?"

"You couldn't compare the two families. My family never travelled all the time. My dad had bought little bits of ground

round Newton Abbot and Plymouth, so we would stop on the commons. Then on to a bit of ground he owned that was about all the travelling we done. All in one area—till he brought us up country to pick the pea fields where I met your dad and broke my own dad's heart."

"It never took me long to realise my mistake," she said. "Right out the frying pan on to the fire. Me and our Ellen was having a hard time with my dad and step-mother but nothing compared with what I had to face with your dad's lot. I was never beaten when living with my dad. Yes he would clip our ears, but never beat us,"

"I couldn't understand their way of life at first," said my mum.

"Always on the move, always shifting on. They were their own masters, and lived a life I never knew of. They bred horses, worked on farms most of the year, went hop picking and out hawking-dropping rag bills to collect scrap. We never collected scrap, but would hawk the seaside towns and villages with fresh wild flowers and brushes, combs, tea, clothes and lace table clothes—that sort of things. It was a different way of life to my own, always on the move and they made clothe pegs and wooden flowers. We had never done that. It was all new and strange to me."

"It must have been very strange, Mum—I mean the difference in the life styles."

"It was past that my Maggie—to me at first your dad's lot was like a pack of wild geese. I could hardly understand a word some of um said. They talked fast to each other and spoke in our language much more than my family did. I caught on quick enough that they talked Romani, thinking I never understood it, but I did you know. I shocked a few of 'um at times with what I did know—which would bring downfall on my head from the old granny. She thought your dad had taught it to me."

"Did you hear that?" she would say in a raised voice. "She's even picking up on our way of talking now. She'll end up trying to run this family before long—slip her halter Lenard and set her going. She's learning our craft and hers to it. Don't bear thinking on—slip her halter my boy before it's too late and send her, and her two bastards packing back to Devonshire."

"I used to slip up in my wagon and have a good laugh to myself of that lot," she told me.

"You were brave mum to stand up for yourself. Bet I couldn't have done it," I told her.

"My dear Maggie, you were born in a temper, born crying so loud, you were heard all over the pea field you were born on and have had a bad quick temper ever since. No, my gal, they would have moured (killed) you quick enough—but I learned to bide my time. My day would come, and it did at times, when I could out hawk them and beg good clothes for my children. And I got myself a little iron ironer that I would heat up in the yog, and after washing and drying your clothes, I would iron it out that used to get up your granny's nose. She hated that and holler the gorgie got her ironing thing out again. Dear lord, what will she get up to next and that little iron brought a bit of joy in to me life because it made your granny jealous. Yes she was jealous over my ironing so you see I did have me bright times. They couldn't quite cow me down."

"I remember that iron, Mum, but I never knew it caused you trouble," I said.

"No, not trouble, my Maggie. I just told you it brought a little joy in to my life. I was out-numbered living with your dad's lot, but not brow beaten. I stood my ground and wouldn't budge an inch, if I did, they would have been much worse to me. And I come from the wrong family to be brow beaten down. No they never had it all their own way with me. If they did, I wouldn't be here today with you now, would I?"

"What about when my dad was in the war mum? How did you manage?"

"It was very hard. Your uncle cripple Jessie made me pegs and wooden flowers. I tried but couldn't get the knack of it so he made me some to keep my head above water. He was good like that and I would make my own crep wax roses and pick cowslips and primroses to sell. Jim would catch me rabbits to cook and some to sell but the nights were the worst after I put you children to bed, I would sit up in the wagon as I would hear the German bombers going over and lay and tremble and shake all night. I would fret on to death in case one landed on us. I only had you and my Alfie, and my little boy I lost was my babe in arms. So yes I was terrified most of the time as a wagon is no match for a bomb and that's all I had. Also, I had to stay round the lanes of Wedmore because that was how your dad could find us. Apart from when Jessie or Jim took me with them pea picking, but your dad would know where to find us to come and check we was still alive. I never knew from one day to the next if he got killed by the bombs in Bristol and he never knew about us. It was a bad time all round. We had years of it, but apart from cripple Jessie, a couple of farmers wives would sell me milk and cheese and homemade bread at that time and an egg or two if I got lucky. They knew I was on my own with my three babies.

"But the heart-breaking thing was, I would take the three of you out hawking, walking miles each day, all round Chedder and Axbridge, meeting house dwellers no better off than myself—to knock on a door only to find they had been delivered the cursed telegram telling them their man or son had been killed in action. That was bad, real bad. I felt for they women. My God I did.

"With hardly any thing in the shops the owners had to serve their own people before us. That's why I relied on two farms that helped me for so long. I shan't forget the two blessed women—they were good to me."

"How did you get on pea picking, Mum?"

"Oh, I drove my own wagon behind who ever took me along with them. We pulled on the headlin of the pea fields to make life easier for us all. I picked on my own till you two got big enough to fill a few buckets a day. I done all right for myself and there was times your dad managed to ride with me for a few weeks in and out—that was a great help—till he got picked up and carted off back to Bristol to the glass house then back on fire watching duty. We had to make the best of our roads, my Maggie. I was lucky I had your uncles to help me out."

"Where did the old granny spend the war, Mum?"

"I think mostly up the Prince lane, with her other sons and daughters. She had her family to help them get by but cripple Jessie stopped not too far from me, as did Jim. They too was a godsend to me in the war years."

"Why didn't they stop with you mum to keep you company," I asked.

"Well my Maggie, they thought if we were all scattered about, and a bomb dropped, at least some of us would live to tell the tale—and it was not right for a married woman to stop with other men and their families as lies could soon break up a family. Although I fret a lot of the time, I preferred it that way."

"And after the war, what did you do then, Mum?"

"Well, the first thing your dad had to do was pack us up and travel to see his mum and dad. When we got to the Prince lane, most of your dad's family was there as they had all had a hard few years but was glad to be alive and kicking to carry on. I told your dad in no uncertain terms that it would only be a day and night. Then he was to pull back on the road again or I would harness up and shift myself. I've finished being got at by your lot, I told him. Enough is enough, I've had to fend for me and my three babies for the past four years. I ain't gonna let your lot shit on me no more."

"Oh dear, Mum, did he get mad at you for your strict talking?"

"No. He never, he knew I was capable of doing what I said I would. Gone was the young foolish gal he married and now we had three babies to work for and keep out of harm's way. We were both young and fit so able to work and earn our living but I would take no more beatings and he knew that and to top it all the war years made him proud of me, for keeping my head above water and coming through it all. Without having him around to help most of the time. Yes, I think that's when I became a woman in his eyes."

"You had a bad life with some of my dad's lot did it get any better after the war?"

"Not really, but your dad began to realise what a nasty old woman his mum was, and he did turn on her, which got him and some of his brothers to come to blows. It nigh on split the family till the poor man Dannal stepped in, and told the old woman that all the rows over me had been down to her and Touie. If you boys wants to fight and kill each other, then get over in that field and do it. Get out of my sights. His sons knew when he meant business and knew better than answer their dad back.

"And as for you two, Emma and Touie cut it out or I'll set about the two of you."

"And did things get any better, Mum?"

"Not really. The dear old man's threats wore off them in time and I told you how I set about Touie and got bound over for a twelve month. We both did in fact, that slowed the old woman down because I told her she would get the same medicine I gave her daughter and I meant every word I said and she knew I could bide my time to get at her. I told them I had lived near the woods to be free of owls."

"So that first meeting after the war never went too well then, Mum?"

"No! Your dad's family was a strange lot—right or wrong, they would stick together. Loved fighting but not shy of hard work but their life style took a bit of getting used to Maggie. But I did in the end. May and Jim were a good help to me. We used to travel a lot with them. They were the happy times, me and May went out hawking every day selling a few gross of pegs or wooden flowers. The best was the wild daffies and snowdrops—they always sold well."

"Did you ever regret having an upcountry man, Mum?"

"Many times in the early days, but when he started to take my side things worked out, and he loved his children with every bone in his body. He made sure you lot never went without anything. Yes, you had a good dad, Maggie."

Chapter 3
Back on the Roads

It was good to be back on the roads again. My dad and Jim were on the lookout for some decent horses to buy to break in to the wagon work. So early spring we were travelling with May and Jim up round Wiltshire way going after the wild daffies. My dad had pulled in by a brook and took off one of the wagon wheels as it was getting very loose in its spokes so he chucked it in the brook to soak and make the wood swell to tighten it up. He would, he said get a new one, the first chance he got. The next day we were travelling along one of the main roads heading for Stour Head and the wild daffies when Jim coming from behind shouted for my dad to pull over.

The velly in the wheel had given out which made the whole thing fall apart. We were in a bit of a mess miles from the nearest village where there was a wheel right. My dad was livid with himself for letting the wheel get so bad.

He blamed himself and was having a good old cuss for the state he found himself in when from far off up the road we heard the clatter of horses' steel shoes hitting the tarmac.

"Lord above don't let that be some other travellers," said my dad, "to catch me in this state of affairs with my wagon like a cockerel on three legs. I'll never live it down," he moaned.

As we all looked back the road to our dismay coming towards us was this high stepping turn out—a big colourful 'Reading wagon' and what a beautiful sight it was, as it was drawn along by a pair of pie bold horses—with a painted up trolley coming on behind it. My poor dad could have died of shame. He was mortified.

As we watched, they came slowly on and pulled up by us.

"I see you got trouble, brother," said a smartly-dressed man. "Can me and my boys be of help to you?"

"Yes," said Jim, "the wheel's given out and we needs to prop up the wagon before it tips over. Thank you for offering we'll be glad of your help." There's my dad glaring at Jim for accepting their help when all he wanted was for the man with the fancy turn out to shift on and not show him up.

Right away we all noticed the man spoke with a London accent. We had heard this accent before up in the hop gardens from the gorgie pickers who came every year (Gorgie is Romani for non-gypsy).

He pulled his wagon off the road on to the grass verge as did his two boys, then off went his jacket ready to help my dad and Jim. One of the boys cut a stout stick out the hedge to prop up the wagon while the other boy, without being told to, took off the remainder of the old wheel.

"Now where's the nearest wheel right?" asked the man.

"Back about five miles," answered Jim. "There's none that I know off ahead of us."

"Well, let's get started," said the man, "and see if we can get you fixed up." He asked one of his boys to pick up the old velly to take with them so that any wheel they found would fit on the wagon ankle, because some carts and wagons had a mixture of sizes when it came to ankles.

It was only when they put their jackets back on that we noticed the strangers wore black arm bands—a sign of a recent death in their family.

"I'm Jim," said Jim, "This is my brother Lenard," and went on to name us all to the new-comers.

"And I'm Liberty, my oldest son Liberty, and my other son is Frankie. My wife is up in the wagon and is called Vashty."

We had not set eyes on the wife since they stopped to help us which was quite unusual as we were all a nosy band of people and liked to see what each other looks like.

"Is your woman bad in bed?" asked my mum. "Can me and May here be of any help to her?"

"It's not as simple as that," he answered with a sad tear in his voice, tapping his arm band. "We lost our only daughter in confinement two months back and my wife can't get over it," then the tear drops fell from his sad eyes and down went his head on to his chest. The two boys too looked sick onto death at their father's words, and both hung their heads in respect of their sister.

"I'm right sorry to my heart to hear your loss," said my dad. "Anything we can do—it's yours for the asking—just say the word and it's done."

"Thank you brother but only the dear Lord can help us now. The baby, a little boy, died as well as my gal so we ended up with a double loss. If only the baby had lived, it would have helped me wife to no end.

"So we pulled out to travel the country like, to get away for a bit and from my son-in-law whose taking it right hard. He and my wife were crying all their days together and it was not doing her any good to stay with him. His family are good friends of ours, said it was for the best to part them from each other. They will take care of their boy and I want what's best for my family and so here we are miles from home giving it our best try."

"Well you must travel with us two lots and we'll give you all the help we can brother." said my dad.

"Right out, Jim?"

"Right out, Lenard," he agreed.

And so the two boys and their dad, with my dad and Jim, drove back the way we had come to sort out a wheel, giving us lot a dire warning not to go anywhere near our wagon in case it tipped over on us. As my mum and May watched the man's trolly go out of sight, May said, "I'll put the kettle on my Vie and you can take that poor little body up a drop of tea, eh."

When my mum went up into the high wooden wagon, we lot hung round the sharves to listen and hear what was being said, but couldn't hear very much—only loud sobbing at times and some of it coming from my mum.

But we did manage to hear my mum ask the question. "My Vashty, when was the last time you cooked your man and boys a meal?"

"I don't know," she said, "I just don't know."

"Well, today is the day for you to start looking after your man and two boys, my gal. So get up and we'll all get the pots and pans on that old yog out there because my Vashty, they three men of yours is suffering too you know and needs your help and grub in their bellies."

When this grieving dear woman come down out her wagon, we all thought what a beautiful looking woman she was—dressed in deep black, with black hair piled on top of her head, she made a sad but beautiful picture.

We older ones ran off to the farmer's trough to fetch clean cooking water and more wood for the yog—my mum and May talking and egging the woman on to peel her spuds and clean a cabbage to cook.

"Come on my babe that's kushti. Let's show our men how well we women can get a meal fit for a king to eat."

After a while, the dear heartbroken woman relaxed and got on with the meal making. Then they shared a tea pot of strong sweet tea while we broke up the wood and fed the yog.

After a while, we heard the clip clop of the horses hoofs coming down the road. On reaching us the man spotted his woman. Just as my mum shook her head at him to act normal like and let her get on with it. He could not believe his eyes nor could their sons as they watched her dish out the four pretty plates full of well cooked food. He looked at me mum and said a silent thank you, then looked up at the sky and said it silently again. He had his woman back at last. The boys, their mother; my mum just gave him one of her special winks telling him all would be well from now on. It would take a long time but all would be well as now they could all share their grief, all four of them.

But it was not quite alright. It is normal that we talk long and sad about someone very dear to us whom we have lost in death. The memories are shared and raked over time and time again. The father and sons would speak of their beloved daughter and sister out of ear shot of his wife, but Vashty would never talk of her gal and her death to any one of us—apart from her husband while in bed. This was not quite right in the eyes of us Romanies. It just don't happen so something was still very wrong with Vashty.

She went on cooking and cleaning—even went out hawking a few wooden clothes pegs with my mum and May but not a mention of her loss.

Her man asked my mum and May, "What is I going to do?" he asked sadly. "Can you two help me and my boys? My boys are sick with worry. It's like they lost their mother as well as their blessed sister"

"What does she say when you both are alone then?" asked May.

"That she wants us to turn back so she can look after our girl's grave. She wants to go home to the yard we got back in London. But I got this fear on me that she'll take to her bed again or have a complete breakdown. Any help you can give us, I would be so grateful because you two have done so much for us already."

"Leave it to us two and we'll give it our best shot," said my mum. "Won't we, May?"

"You can bet your sweet life, we will," smiled May.

In a few days, we were back on the old road heading for the little wild daffie woods. It was good to be travelling again because me and our Alfie and our two cousins Jimmy and Lilea, May and Jim's two eldest, loved new stopping places to pull on. We always found exciting things to explore and mud or cow troughs to play with or in. If I was truthful, we played under the watchful yocks of a herd of cows, who would bellow at us to push off and play elsewhere and leave them in peace to chew the cud. Cheeky sods! We liked the cows as they always smelt of warm fresh milk but they never liked us playing in their fields.

Then we got to the daffie woods and once unpacked we all sat round the kushti yog while my dad taking Liberty with him went to hunt out the gamekeeper who was known to us. As I explained in *Our Forgotten Years*, this gamekeeper would only let certain Travellers pick the little wild flowers because of his game bird breeding thingy he did deep in the huge woods. He would threaten to shoot any dogs that got into his wood and that's why ours was tied up good and proper for the few days we would be here picking the flowers that grew in abundance deep in the wood.

In a short while, with the gamekeeper in tow, our two men came back.

"Yes we could have just a couple of days picking, that's if everyone behaved themselves and never disturbed his birds, namely his pheasants and wild ducks. This was a very strict man who meant every word," he said.

"First sign of trouble and it would be us lot in the trouble," he told us.

But he had known my dad and his family for many years and always let them have a fair few days picking—"It is up to you, Jim, and you Lenard, to keep your kids and dogs under control" was his last warning to us. Then he was gone through the gap in the wood and vanished—him and his twelve bore gun. That gun scared the shit out of us all because we knew he would use it if shove come to push.

Vashty couldn't wait to see and pick her first wild daffies. My mum on pretence of warning us to behave told us that we four older ones was to stick close to aunt May—well away from her and aunt Vashty.

"I wants to talk to her private like. Out of ear shot of you lot, got that?" she asked us.

"Yes, Mum, we got it." My mum was up to something and we four knew it.

So with the three women, we four, dragging our pillow slips which we had to store the picked flowers in, started our long trek in to the big old wood where we knew of old where the flowers grew. They only grew in certain parts of the wood.

Each year when we come to pick the flowers, I knew what I would see but each and every year the very sight of the huge spreads of flowers, and odd clumps among the bushes always took me breath away. Like a div, I just had to stand and take in this beautiful sight of nature at its best.

Take heed dear reader of this book. If you ever get the chance to visit Stourhead Woods in early spring, you could have your breath fair taken out of your body. On first sight of these fantastic wild flowers, you would never regret it.

Aunt May had to poke me in the back to get me moving. I couldn't for the life of me take my yocks off this beautiful sight.

"Come on my little Maggie, let's pick over here," and she herded us four away from my mum and Vashty. It was some time later when we heard Vashty cry out and turned to run where she and my mum were picking.

"Oh no you don't," said May, "you four get yer head down and ass up and keep on picking the flowers or no treats for you lot come tomorrow."

Looking to where my mum and Vashty were, we saw Vashty sat on the cold ground crying her heart out and my mum patting her shoulder but we could not hear what they were saying or talking about.

After we had picked our fill, we met up and started to make our way back to the gap and the wagons. My mum winked at May with a secret meaning to it. All she hoped for had gone well with whatever she had been up to with poor Vashty, and Vashty was hugging something in her headscarf tight to her chest.

As soon as we got back, the hot tea was being drunk by everyone with my mum giving Liberty knowing looks, and he hung his head.

My mum, who could never keep quiet, said softly, "Liberty, your Vashty got something to show you and the boys." The dear woman looked at my mum with pain-filled yocks.

"Oh, and what's that then, my Vashty," asked Liberty.

"Vie there helped me dig up a handful of these flower bulbs to put on our girl's grave, my Lib. We can keep them till we get back home again," she said. "They would grow on her grave and flower every year, ain't that so, my Vie?"

"Yes, my Vashty—your gal will love that. A little bit of Wiltshire growing on her dear bit of grave. Yes she'll like that, and when you plant them you can tell her of us travelling and picking the daffies together. She would like that as well."

And so it was these beautiful little wild flowers that opened a grieving mother's heart, just open enough to speak of her beloved lost daughter. And to start talking of her beloved daughter, not a great deal at first, but the dam broke over the coming weeks, giving that family a little sad peace in their lives.

This family gave us news, or call it information, because up in this big London they talked of, there was a good many travelling families living in their own little yards, doing all kinds of jobs to earn a living. And since they lived for many generations among the gorgie population, they had picked up some of our Romani language, and would use words such as Kuahti, Vonger and Chore. This cracked our men up, and there was much laughter going on around our yog—gorgies speaking our language, "Never in this world," laughed Jim.

Yes they do, and we don't mind them using the odd word or two because we all get along and trust each other. We, like our dads before us, have grown up with these people, and can't see any difference in each other. They accepted us lot for who we are long, long ago and have been coming down to Kent with us for donkey's years to pick the hops and apples and things. No my friends, the gorgies and us lot get on right well back up in the smokey town.

"Well, they don't accept or use any of our language round our part of the country, Liberty. By God, they don't and what about your gavers? How do they treat you?" asked Jim.

"No different to the rest of the people. They treat us the same way as they treat the gorgies. If you do a crime, you pay the fine. That's it really."

"They don't call you bad and dirty names, or kick your yog over you then?" asked my dad.

"No," answered Liberty. "We don't get any of that kind of treatment. Some ain't as nice as others, but on the whole we get treated well."

So this told our lot that it was only while travelling the roads that the gaver mushes practised abuse and at times violence. It really was hard to believe it could be so different stopping in a town. It just goes to show that people could be reasonable to others if they had a mind to, but not so it seems out in the countryside.

Weeks later, it was time to shake hands and say farewell to a lovely family. They were heading home to tend to that little mother and baby grave and to learn that life still goes on, no matter what sorrow we have to face. That's Gypsy life.

My dad and Jim tried their hardest to get them to come to a pea picking, but it was turning back time for them, and for us the pea fields would soon be waiting to be picked. And my mum and May were given a new mat each for their wagons because this family were London carpet sellers and had brought a few mats with them to sell. We never saw or heard from this family again, but there was one little chick that was pleased; some of our daffies would live up in London, and that certain chick was me.

Over the past weeks, we had learned a lot about life way up in this London place, as to how hard and frightening it was during the war years. When whole streets were bombed to the ground all around their yard and how they spent most nights in an air raid shelter, thinking it would be their last night on earth.

And when told that we never had an air raid shelter to run to, they could not make out how we survived. Although very frightening at the time, we were much safer way out in the countryside and lucky to boot to have scrapped through.

They told us of the young men, Romani Gypsy men, who fought for the king and country; and named the ones who never made it back, and the ones who did, of the devastation of those families who lost husbands and sons and not a grave to sit by. No, they were buried abroad. That was a double blow to the Romani families, because our graves become a focus point.

"To be kept covered in flowers out of respect," he told of one mother who would not accept that her son was never coming back. How she watched the road waiting for him to come walking round that bend and home.

"God willing, my boy will come back to us," she would cry.

"Sad old times," my dad answered.

And the nights we all sat round the roaring yog and my dad trying to chop out for Liberty's turnout. "My brother," he said, "I could never get rid of my old wagon, because my dear old dad had it made for me and my woman when we got married. It was a wedding gift, so it will stay in my family till it falls apart."

"Fair play to you, Liberty. I would feel the same as you if it were mine," said my dad.

They asked us to travel back with them and have a few months stopping on their yard.

"Thank you all the same," said Jim, "but my brother, we lot could never live in a big town. We would surely pine away for the open roads."

"I understand, and I think you are right as you wouldn't like our ways in the town. It's not your kind of life. No, you lot would be like caged birds. We were bred and born into it so it is our kind of life but it's nice to get out of it once in a while. We told you how we come out to pick the hops and peas in Kent and then make our way back up again."

We had heard of hop picking in Kent but never had a clue as to where Kent was. It meant little to us, as in those days, we only knew our own travelling route and never strayed far from it, but had it not been for a broken wheel, we may never have met these good and honest people. They had shared our lives for a few months; then they were gone out of our lives forever. Having left us with memories of our travelling friends we shared with others, for long years, around our yog after night-fall.

Chapter 4
The Pea Fields

And so the month of May was looming round the bend, and our little group headed for Bridgwater back down in Somerset—and the pea and broad bean fields, much as we always did at this time of the year. Looking forward to a couple of months' paid work and a safe place to stop on.

Because we would be meeting up with maybe a hundred families, the wagons were spruced up with a lick of paint. The horses washed and rubbed with a handful of straw or dried grass till they would shine like glass bottles—rules again. You always kept things in a clean and tidy order, because everything we owned was on full view to others.

We got down as far as the outskirts of Glastonbury and pulled round the lanes under the Tor—these are very pretty lanes with moss and grass growing in the middle of the lane, with high hedges full of Hazel bushes and Elder and stringy Elm. The narrow verges covered in sweet grass and herbs for our horses to eat and we four older ones had plenty of exciting things to do and play with. For the few days we were there, we four climbed right up to the top of the tor from which we could see most of the world, or so we thought. At the top was this stone built house, without doors or windows that you could see out of. It was a queer old place, but we loved to roll topsy-turvy back down to the field area. Full of young energy, we would scramble back up time after time, as we knew that big tump with the skinny house on top very well. Having been stopping here for past years, it was the well-known "Glastonbury Tor" as it is known today.

Then we found ourselves passing slowly through the town of Bridgwater. This town would benefit greatly from the pea pickers every Saturday, from the families doing their weekly shopping and the men in the pubs, spending like there was no tomorrow. Throwing the beer down their long necks—so it was not with dismay the shop keepers watched as the wagons passed through their town. For the wagons meant coins spilling through their fingers into the tills.

Stopping on the grass verge near the pea grower's farm that we chose to pick for, the men went off to find out where we were to pull in for the season. When they came back, they gave the women a choice—either they could pull in the farm paddock for the season, or follow the pea field headland known to us as 'headlin'. Thus, it was decided, we two lots would follow the headlins from field to field as we picked them clean of peas or beans.

It would make life easier for them with small children to cope with the early morning starts—for 4 a.m. was the normal starting of their day. Stopping on the headlin, the children could be left to sleep till 7 a.m. when we stopped for breakfast; whereas, in the farm paddock, the children had to be dragged out of bed still sound asleep and took out to the fields. This was a hard time on the young children, but my mum and May would have none of it. It was either the headlin, or they would come out on the field after the youngsters woke up and miss the best part of the pea picking day. So it was the headlins for us, because both May and my mum had young children to think of, and we just loved stopping on the headlins where we had our homes and horses right there in the work area with us. And our men would have a good headstart on the families that had to travel to the fields. Bit crafty, but it all bode well for us little lot.

The first day picking was always fun and work. With Jimmy and Lilea tucked on the outside of their dad and me, and our Alfie tucked on the outside of my dad to keep us apart while we picked in our tin buckets and not fall behind playing the goat like we used to do while on the roads.

We four were given a row of peas each to pick, while the grown-ups took up to five or six rows as their lot to pick. If any of us four got left behind, sparks could fly. We were now part of the workforce and had to hold our end up. I was about six at this time, but had been picking peas since I was about three years old; so was well used to it, and to top it all, I was one of many children who had been born on a pea headlin or in the farm paddock. We were born pickers and took it in our stride as part of our way of life style.

There's nothing quite like the sight of a new unpicked pea field. Peas are grown in rows and spread right across the whole field. The hedges were full and green, and the headlin, which went right round the field, was sprouting wild flowers. I've always appreciated nature and could see beyond the growing of peas, beans and hops. To most of my community, it was just vegetable or hop gardens or whatever kind of field we were working on. But I could notice the difference in colours such as the lighter green of the growing peas, to the darker green and browns of the hedges surrounding it, to the different big old trees. Each with a colour of their own, and the woods, cops and spinnys. The different colours of the mosses and tree trunks, everything has its own identity if you look close enough, and I could spot them all. Nature is one of our greatest free gifts and should be enjoyed and taken notice of.

Sometimes, I would ask my dad a question, "Why is that tree like that and that other tree looks like that or…" Some such question.

"My Maggie, you're the oddest child I have ever known. Go and fetch some wood. The trees are just trees. Now fetch that wood."

So he thought I was odd. Maybe, I was a bit odd, who knows, but it makes one wonder. Our lot travels all over the countryside and sees everything there is to see. Yet in truth, they see nothing, because it's always been there and part of their everyday lives. Things, as far as they are concerned, are where they should be, that is until a farmer grubs out a hedge. Now they are the first to take notice that a hedge is gone, where a hedge should have been. So maybe, just maybe, they do see things but don't notice till they're gone. Who knows, because my lot is a queer funny old lot of people.

But me, I'm a nature baby and enjoy all the changes in the seasons. I can see beauty in a leaf-covered tree and beauty in a naked tree in winter.

I used to think my dad was the wisest person I knew, but then I think of my mum. For such a small made person, and I must say a very pretty one, people took to her. They would seek out her advice and help, and it would be given willingly and taken note of. I enjoyed the days she took me out hawking with her, and the things she would say to me such as—

"Maggie, see that blue door up ahead? Give that door a miss. Don't call on it."

"Why?" I would ask.

"Because, I told you so. There is sickness in that house. Now give it a miss."

How would she know there was sickness in that house? We hadn't been in this village for months.

Yes, I think I had a wise mother as well as my dad.

4 a.m. out on the peas, big fat sweet juicy peas, two for the bucket, one for me. I must have eaten nearly a net full on that first day as we all did. However, as the days panned out, you would hardly bother to stop and shell a pea to eat raw but had them cooked for every meal, till the peas came out of their ears. As I look back, there were many good times in our lives and pea picking was one of the best. Family and friends gathered on weekends and some evenings to catch up on a year's chit chat. It was a grand time, to just sit on an upturned bucket and hear all the news and banter going on around the yog. We did not need to keep us warm, but for cooking and kettles as it was the centre of our stopping place. A spot to gather around—everyone headed for the yogs and spilled what they knew of others of our community. And one bit of news made our men prick up their ears that there was to be a fist fight coming Sunday morning in a field on another pea farm. 5 am in the morning, they would meet and fight it out. It was all over a deal, we were told. One "fore sharped" the other on a deal with a third person, meaning he witnessed a deal being discussed, then went behind the others back and dealt for whatever it was for himself. Hence the coming punch up, which my dad and Jim would go to watch and be late getting out on the pea field. Sunday was classed as the first day of the weeks—picking peas ready for Monday market.

This was a time in our working lives we had everything our hearts desired, if the weather was kind, and that particular year it was being very kind to us all. We were earning a few quid, had plenty to eat and drink and us children were getting as brown as berries. Then we had the travellers who came to visit us in evenings on horseback or driving carts or trolleys. But the weekends could get a bit rough and wild, old scores had to be settled so organised fist fights was fought. The winner shaking hands with his challenger or vice versa, weddings that had been planned for a few years, where the drinks flowed like water, and a few disagreements later a black yock or two were worn like medals. It all went on, but come Sunday morning, 4 am saw them back out on the pea field. As I said, Sunday was the starting of a new week, very little, if any, was picked on a Friday. It meant that Friday and Saturday was our weekend so with a few battered and bruised Sundays or no Sunday, we were back at work. Getting a few nets of peas entered in the farmer's book for Friday's payday.

It made us laugh to hear the groans from hangovers.

"Oh, my poor head."

"I'll never drink again, not ever."

But on the next Sunday, the groans would be back—self-inflicted groans yes, we had much to laugh about when dozens of families worked the same spread of peas or broad beans.

I look back on these days as some of the happiest times of my life. Wild, carefree days, no gavers could shift us on. We earned a few shillings or more each day. New babies coming in to our world, weddings, trips in to the town of Bridgwater—that really was a treat. Fresh cooked pigs, trotters, or fish and chips wrapped in old newspapers—that was high living after days out on the fields bending up and down. A million times a day pulling up the pea allum to strip it off its peas.

Sadly, it all began to fizzle out. The peas were nearly all picked and netted and then sold. The broad beans long gone—it was nearly time to pull out and head up north to Ledbury and the hop gardens.

Aunt May and my mum voted to give Bridgwater Fair a miss, so did Jim. It was left for them to convince my dad to do the same but he was stubborn and it was hard work to get him to change his mind. He really wanted to stay for the horse fair and dug his heels in. He was going to that fair, come rain or shine, or so he thought.

But my mum had the few quid that they had worked so hard for out on the peas which were tucked away safe and sound but knew it would not be at all safe if my dad got to that fair.

"Tell you this then, my Len," said my mum, "we'll share out the vonger (money) we earned out on the fields. You take your half to the fair, and I'll take me and my babies in the wagon up to Hereford. We'll see you come Christmas, now what do you think on that."

"YOU, you bitch, you...you think I'd let you take my children, hoss and wagon up to Hereford? Over my dead body I will."

"Then you better come with us. That money ain't burning a hole in your pocket—well go on and spend it—and I'll top my share up on the hops—a dinalow and his vonger is soon parted," was her parting shot.

"You would too, wouldn't you? You would take everything we own and leave me on the side of the road. Wouldn't you? You pretty dear," he said grinding his teeth.

He went to grab my mum but Jim stepped in and caught hold of my dad.

"Don't you hit her, my brother. I don't want to knock you down but I will if you hit that little body. Her and your lot been working their guts out on the peas as you have. Now give her a fair crack of the whip. She's earned it."

"Come on my brother let's have a drop of sloppy (tea) and talk it out. Put the kettle on my May," he told her. "We got to chat about this thing."

And chat they did till my dad begrudgingly had to give way but he was now not on speaking terms with any one of us. As we packed up and put out the yog, he kept his peace. Mumbling he would not pick one 'ffing hop even if it killed him. On his life he wouldn't.

And so, breathing a sigh of relief, we set off up the old A38 on our long trek to the area of Hereford. In deadly silence I might add, but after stopping for a night and shifting on again, he started to sing to himself while driving his horse. "If I had my way dear, you would never grow old and sunshine I would bring every day," he sung his song over and over till we all joined in including my mum, Jim and May, and their children. It was quite a noisy little band that passed through a quiet village, in fact we were as happy as sand larks and the row was forgotten and buried. My mum had won round one but round two was waiting in the form of a local pub near to the hop gardens and me crafty dad knew it. Boy would he wet his whistle next weekend. He could be read like a book, could my dad he had given in far too easy for our liking. He had something up his sleeve, the crafty sod.

My mum had made more ground with my dad. Over the past couple of years he knew she was capable of jumping on that Devonshire bound train so he had kept his hands to himself. Oh yes, he would make threats but knew better than to carry them out. He also knew my mum could cling to vonger like glue. She would have a good bit put bye, hidden deep somewhere—where no matter how much he searched for it, it never came to light. He would have a rummage in the wagon when we were out calling. Our Alfie had whispered it to my mum what he was up to so she was well aware of his capers and was always one step ahead of him. Money and my dear old dad soon parted company as the old saying goes.

But he was a good dad, one of the very best and loved us all dearly. He worried and cared for us night and day. We knew he would lay down his life for his little family. Faults or no faults, he was our dad and the main stay of our family and that's how we all held him, as our protector and head of our unit. Our king you might say.

There was no doubt who his queen was—he was proud of my mum. Even when she had to brain him when he was drunk as a skunk which she did from time to time. We thought she would be the death of him one day but he survived till his eighties. They both did in fact. God rest and bless them both. The road leading us up to the hop country could be full of pitfalls—it was a route used by hundreds of us and the gavers were right on their toes ready to keep us on the move. They had their orders and we had our horse's welfare to think of. Pulling a heavy wagon up hill and down for up to fifteen miles a day was enough hard work for them. They too needed food and a rest so it was a battle of wills and much losing of tempers most of the time. Jim who was not so quick tempered as my dad, usually did the talking when the gavers came up on us.

Mind you, in all fairness to the Romani men, the attitude of the police played a big part in our dislike and distrust of them. Some would turn up like their life depended on moving us on like bulls in a china shop—all mouth and trousers as my dad would say while others would be more human and sociable. But the law had the upper hand and was to be obeyed or a few nights in the lock up and a hefty fine was the price for answering back. My dad hated the police. All his life he and many others of our community hated the police. I don't think true trust will ever grow between my community and the law. The reason being, for many generations we were persecuted by the law-harsh words you may think but true all the same. Just think in them days the police used pushbikes or horses to find out where we were stopping at. There was no police radios or cars with phones in them. It was a full head on meeting with no witnesses on our side of the fence. They cared not for our culture or customs or life style and no matter what happened or what attitude they used on our families, the police was always in the right. Unlike today when we have the right to put in a complaint against them back beyond the forties and fifties it was not heard of, if it was we knew not about it. So it was a battle of wills between the Gypsies and the police force and some battles could get bloody. My dad and others of our race would and did have fist fights with some of the police. Their uniform was no barrier if they took up a fist fight challenge from our men. It was a man to man fight and, I must say, mostly enjoyed on both sides but it did happen on occasion. The police today would never dream of throwing off his helmet and getting stuck in, making blood and snot fly in all directions and I think a few had a surprise when they found themselves on a losing end of the stick. Our men were no push overs—fit and strong from field work and all the walking and other hard work they carried out. They knew at times the police officer would meet his match but for all the shouting and blasting, in the end we had to shift on.

Me dads brother Cripple Jessie was the man who feared no one. He would fight any police man who would take up the challenge. This is very true, I have a letter from an old police officer telling me of the fights with cripple Jessie, and to be fair Jessie used his driving whip while the officer used his truncheon. I must explain a driving whip was made out of whale bone covered in fine leather at the handle end of the whip was either a silver knob or a heavy brass knob to give the whip a fine finish and a good hand grip. And Jessie would use the end with the knob on to crack the copper on top the head with or at least loosen a few teeth. He was a right character, my uncle Jessie, and brazen with it.

All my dad's seven brothers could handle themselves but it was Jessie and my dad who got into most of the fights. The others would join in if needed and enjoyed doing so. They in their own right was a force to be reckoned with but a great bunch of brothers. It was all for one and one for all. Their way of life put them in all sorts of situations that had to be dealt with one way or another.

I must explain—fist fighting was used to settle a dispute. This is a very old custom going back hundreds of years not none of your dirty fighting. It was an organised event—boots and rings removed and one man to see fair play. The fight would be fair and bloody but the two men would always shake hands and give best to the winner when the fight was over and be friends again till the next time that is.

And here we are with two well-built gavers standing by our yog telling us to pack up and move on.

The look on my dad's face was a picture. He had just unharnessed his horse after a long old pull up hill and down. He was flabbergasted, couldn't the gaver see the horses was all sweated up, in fact you could smell it coming off their hot bodies.

"Leave this to me," said Jim, fearing my dad was going to blow his top and upset two already angry gavers.

"Sir," said Jim, "we only just pulled in, our horses needs to cool down and rest."

"That's your problem! Now get packed up and move on. We don't want the likes of you dirty thieving lot here. We have had enough of you Gypsies stopping wherever you want to. Well not on my patch you don't. Now get moving."

Oh dear, poor Jim got shoved aside by my dad, my mum telling my dad to keep quiet. "My Len kakker let it atch," she was speaking in our Romani language whereas officer thought she was cursing him.

He threatened to run my mum in to the lock up for breach of peace and threatening behaviour.

Jim shouted for us lot to start packing our things. "Hurry my chavvies (children) or there's murders to be done here today."

"Get a move on."

My dad had his jacket off by now and was challenging out the two law men. Snap! He was hand cuffed and being led away up the road, the law pushing their bikes with my dad in-between them, with my dad hollering orders to us over his shoulder.

This is what happened when faced with bad attitude from the law. They can call us all the bad names under the sun and we are not allowed to answer back or, like my dad, it's a handcuff job. Our men for many generations were not treated as men by most of the law men who did their best to belittle and make fun of them in front of their families and, worse still, in front of the settled community at every opportunity they got. Giving the settled community the impression we were all bad people and not to be trusted.

We have even been told by farmers who needed workers that the police had requested they not employ the Gypsies but the farmers had told the law they could employ who they liked and that the Gypsies were a reliable hard working bunch. This made the law of them days more determined to punish us at every chance they got as not all the village officers but most of them.

"Well," said Jim. "Our Lenard will be locked up for the night. We best move on and bail him out in the morning. What a waste of five bob my Vie and so with my mum driving our wagon, we went on through the village and stopped about a mile on the other side of it but come morning, it kicked off again. My mum and Jim had gone at 10 o'clock to bail out or pay his fine at the lock up."

On seeing the state of my dad, my mum let fly saying to the officer,

"One of you never done that to my man—no sir one on his own couldn't serve my man that bad."

My dad had black eyes and holding his side with his hand had been kicked with heavy boots. He was in a right mess and had a job to walk. He had been served bad. If my dad had been in a fair fight with a good fist fighting man, he still would not be in this state. Moreover, he had lost face, he been beaten up by the gavers he hated and felt mortified in front of us lot.

Having paid his fine and a few choice words to the police mush, they took my dad to the village Doctor. On seeing the state he was in, and after his examination finding two broken ribs, mass of cuts and bruises, and a few stiches later, he asked how it happened.

On being told that it happened at the police station, three gavers had set about him, using their boots on him. The Doctor shook his head sadly as there was nothing to be done. My dad had to rub it in and get over it—the law was the law and there were once again no witnesses.

But my dad had one laugh on them—after being in the hop gardens for quite a few weeks and making our way back, we learned that one of the officers involved had passed away. "Where's he buried at," asked my dad.

"Why," asked the mush who told him.

"So I can piss on his grave, the no good bastard."

The mush laughed at this and told my dad.

"You and many more like you would like to do that."

"Oh yes they would."

After a few weeks we pulled on the field set aside by the hop grower for his Traveller pickers. There were huge piles of fire wood and a standpipe for water. We picked a corner and placed the wagons to make our yog more private like.

Whenever a lot of us was together working on the lands, we had our own set of rules that was strictly abided by.

No one visited another family at meal times—this was a private family time.

Children were not allowed to go near any other family's yog, wagon or tent, if the family was not there.

Children were not allowed to run or play in the part of the field where all the horses were kept—nasty life-threatening accidents could happen.

No children were allowed to play with the tap or standpipe of water, as it would make mud and upset the farmer mush.

Men and women had their own area where they went to the loo, as it was forbidden for either sex to break that rule. If they did, they would be thrown off the field by the other travellers, not that this ever happened. We all knew this rule.

No young girl or boy was allowed out of sight together. This was again a very strict rule, they had to stay in sight of family members at all times, which made courting a not very enjoyable time but rules are rules in my community.

There were so many such rules, but we kept to them and were taught right from wrong at an early age. So to us young ones, it was part of our life style. This is something the settled community knew nothing about—if they had, they may have seen us in a different light. They had been educated to think we were a wandering lawless band.

My dad, now his ribs had healed, could once again take over the reins of his family. The night before we were to enter the hop garden, he and Jim gave us young ones a lecture: we were to behave and pick the hops, fetch lighting wood for the yog we would make out in the garden for cooking. We had breakfast and dinner in the garden, tea back at the wagons.

Fetch cans of water and if need be, look after the babies of the family. These lectures come at us, no matter what kind of work we did. We were well used to being kept in order and we were not allowed to go over to the farm yard. This was one of its busiest times of the year and tractors were spinning in and out of sheds and all over the place, it was a dangerous place to be.

To be fair to all parents, their life was spent on keeping their children safe. Life on the road could be full of pitfalls, rivers, deep ponds, cars driving fast round bends all manner of danger could be found or it could find us unsuspecting playing children.

Each year would find new families out in the hop gardens and these folks found us as interesting as we found them. They came from places we had never heard of and had many unheard tales to tell us which was a delight in its self. With one such family, my dad pushed by my mum chopped out our wagon for another. My mum had spotted it as it came a slowly through the gateway, and thought it would suit her down to the ground.

"Dick there, my Len," she said as the wagon came to a chosen spot on the field, "That's as good a wagon as I've seen for many a day. It was a large square bow wagon complete with new sheet covering it. What I'd give to own that my Len." It took several days haggling but my mum got her wagon—it was to be in our family for many years—and she double dared my dad to ever chop it away. It had good cupboard space, a nearly new little iron queenie stove and it was lined with very pretty material under its canvas sheet. All in all it was a sturdy well-made wagon and it was my mum's. She was cock proud the day they swopped over wagons and looked after it so well, it was always as clean and tidy as a new pin.

The first day out on the hop garden always took time to get adjusted to the new work. My dad as usual giving me and our

Alfie all the daft flannel under the sun to keep us at it and making sure we both picked on opposite sides of the hop crib so we couldn't get fighting. This is because me and that brother of mine would fight each other like two march hares. Some days you couldn't count the number of times we came to blows—we could fight over a stone in the road.

I have described the hop gardens in *Our Forgotten Years* but can't help me self-writing about my first sight of it each year. Hop gardens is like no other kind of work we do in the seasons for picking up spuds, picking peas, beans and swede topping is done in open fields where one at times can see for miles. But on entering the hop garden, it's like walking into a live green tunnel with just the skylight to show you the way. But once a space is cleared of the hop vines, then you can see the hedges surrounding it but only behind you as you work your way up the heavy dense rows. The hops is trained to grow up wires and poles and is very high off the ground. The picker has to grab a vine and pull it down over the crib to pick off the hops—big fat green juicy hops—they hang like huge big bunches of grapes. It is a fascinating sight on first entering the garden as it looks spooky in the early misty daylight and when the vines is pulled down, you get showered in wet mist. And it can get you feeling cold and chilled if not dressed up for it—especially when the cold drops runs down your neck like freezing fingers, the more you complain the more your dad gives you loads of old buck to keep picking. If we had everything he promised us, you would need a big old hay wagon to carry it back, but still the promises carried on.

"Come on, Maggie, my baby gal, it's new shoes come Saturday for you." It could be anything from pigs trotters to ice cream, the promises never stopped and slowly we picked on, anything for a bit of peace.

We Romani children had a full childhood but was more grown up in many ways to the children of the settled community. From an early age, we could ride horses, bare back, always bare back; saddles were for the settled dwelling house people. We could drive a horse and cart and even a wagon if it came to it. We had learned how to treat and care for horses and dogs, how to catch a rabbit or sniff out a hedgehog, what herbs to pick for the dads to make potions and herbs and berries our mum's made medicine out of, or berries for dye making. It was a natural part of our lives. We learned about wild animals and birds as we learned to walk and talk and thought every one we met who was non Romani knew the same things, but very few did, as me and our Alfie found out when my mam put us in one of the old schools. All Gypsy children were taught and brought up in the same way as we two were. We were taught to appreciate the free things in life, such as fast running; clean, fresh spring water; and the hedge rows that provided us with wood for the yog; hazel for peg making; elder for medicine and dye and the sticks to whittle out the beautiful wooden chrysanthemum flowers, black thorn for its berries, bramble for the black berries we picked to sell— and the fields that grew tons of wild mushrooms that we also picked to sell. And not least the wild flowers that grew so thick and fast in banks, hedgerows and in woods and fields. There for anyone to pick and enjoy or like us to pick and sell round the villagers' doors. The hop garden also brought us in to close contact with the gorgie pickers from London, Birmingham and other big towns. We watched as the children got adjusted to sleeping and eating in cow sheds or some such place, instead of the warm soft bed and home they had left to work the hop gardens. Most mum's tried to convince us that, they were giving the kids a holiday, but the way they threw themselves into the hop picking proved they were there to earn much needed money—the same as us lot really. The difference was that they had left their homes, we had ours with us, which gave us no hardships—we had our comforts on hand. I've told in *Our Forgotten Years* how our families would feed the little gorgie children—we still did each year we travelled up and got to know a few mothers over the years, and always looked out for them to appear at the farm. But we never met off the garden, they would not come on to our camping field and we never ventured on the farm.

All the travellers enjoyed the hop picking—meeting relatives they only saw once a year on the gardens. Old friends got together and took the world apart round the yogs at night—and told old or fascinating new tales. My dad's mishap with the gavers was greatly discussed and if all the curses came true, the two gavers would be in purgatory serving out their time. No one liked what happened to my dad, it was not fair play at all and with it my dad's hate for the law grew, encouraged by the other men.

This year it was a peaceful season—hardly a miss word spoken every one lived in harmony just as it should be. The weekend drinking and dancing and singing went on week after week—so it was a very happy bunch of travellers all singing from the same hymn sheet for once and a great mixed bunch they were at that. All too soon it was over for another year—wagons tents was made ready to go to many different parts of the country. The farmer came and thanked us for the hard work and said we were all welcome to return the following season.

May and Jim was getting ready to take the long drag back to Wiltshire. We would travel as we come and travel back together, happy as sand larks with the money earned did I get that pair of new shoes, no I never but maybe next year, eh.

But my mum had her new wagon. May had a bit of ware from the china shop in Ledbury and my dad and Jim felt quite rich with the money from the peas and hops and so the occupants of both wagons could be heard singing the old songs as we travelled along. All they wanted was to get back safe and sound and secure some winter work plus fodder for their horses. On and on we went day after day—till we come to the village where my dad got his ribs broke by men of the law and that's where we learned one of them had passed away. It was the butcher mush who told my dad and Jim.

Not that many of the dwelling house folks had too much sympathy for him; he was known, they said, as a bully. Did my dad piss on his grave, I can't answer that one, for in truth I did not know as it wouldn't have been discussed in front of us young ones because we had been taught to respect the dead.

And so our horses slowly trod their way in to Wiltshire, going from farm to farm seeking winter work but not getting much luck. Others had beat them to it.

"We'll try one more, then head down to Somerset," said Jim. "It's time to check on the old uns anyway." He meant the old granny and dear old granddad.

Oh dear, my mum's face said it all—back to the old granny meant her peaceful life would end but we must we supposed.

"You are right our Jim," said my dad.

"We ain't seen hide nor hair of them for months, so let's head back." That was it, we were now making our way back to the Prince Lane and as far as me mam and May was concerned, we was heading right in to the lion's den. For my granny ruled the lane and her dislike of my mum would rear its ugly head and get her and my dad at it—so it was very quiet and the air between my mum and dad was not too kushti.

But it's again an old custom to care for the elderly; my dad knew and the rest of his family knew that we could not spend more than a couple of nights pulled on me granddads own stopping place. Afore trouble flared like a house on fire—between my mum and the old granny—but my dad just had to show his face and although heavy-hearted for what was in store for us, he made for the Prince Lane.

Chapter 5
Family at War

We stopped off at Chippenham—and got a bit of shopping and new shoes for all our horses from the blacksmiths forge. Then we went on towards Bath to one of our favourite stopping places 'Chapple Plaister'.

How well we knew this beautiful common land—it had everything we needed. It was a kushti place to stop, safe for the children to run wild and play and grazing for our horses—a spring of fast running water and a big old bluebell wood from which we got the wood to keep our yog going—as it was a split common. It was cut in to two parts by having a narrow little road going from top to bottom running through it. We had a choice which side of the road we could pull on but always pulled if we could at the top end nearest the main drag on the right hand side—which meant we young ones never had to cross any roads to fetch wood and cans of water. It was a safety measure put in place for the younger children—the grownups always kept in mind the safety of their children and horses wherever they pulled in—yet one more rule.

And to top off our joy of being on the common was the sight of other families already stopping there. One family was Andrew and Dhinea Bowers who had many young children, as I could not count me numbers back then it seemed they had a huge lot of chavvies. We had travelled and picked hops and peas with the Bower family many times over, and enjoyed their company. They were the salt of the earth me dad would say, and that's high praise to give a family—it said it all.

Then we spotted my dad's brother cripple Jessie and his family which was no surprise because this was his favourite part of the country and he spent most of his life in and around the out skirts of Chippenham.

So before we could unpack our few things, both men strolled over to us. Andrew was very pleased to see us again and shook hands with Jim and my dad, saying hello to us all. But the look on my Uncle Jessie's face didn't bode well. He was in an angry mood on sight of his two brothers, which meant trouble—and it never took long for him to start.

"So you two handy objects have decided to show your faces," he said to Jim and my dad. "No matter about me poor old mum and dad then, they could be dead and stiff for all you two cared—months you been gone and not one word have we had from you."

"Hold on big mouth," said my dad. "Yes we been away, but we been following the work, we both got families to feed and water, and now we're making our way back to the lane to me mum and dad, what's it got to do with you what we two do anyway, you with your big mouth."

"If you cared as much for my mum and dad as you do that painted doll you got, they might see more of you."

Oh dear, painted doll was a nick name the old granny had given my mum because she wore make up which made it clear as a bell. My mum had the blame for my dad's not paying humble pie to his old mother.

"You leave my woman out of this, she ain't stopped me doing nothing. Now get back to your wagon afore I makes you," hollered my dad.

In a spilt second, Jessie had his jacket and shirt off and was sparring his fist at my dad. Jim tried to get between them, but was pushed out the way by one or other of the now fighting mad brothers. At it they went, as everyone on the common stood back and watched two brothers beat the shit out of each other. We all knew from previous fights these two had fought that it would be a long fight as neither brother would give in.

And so it went on, as one was knocked down, the other would pull him up and punch the day lights out of him again. There would be no winner or loser in this fight, because they would fight till they could fight no more and be bad friends for months if not years to come.

After a long old time, Jim grabbed my dad and Andrew collared Jessie and parted them, but both fighting cocks was still threatening the other—and all because of my old granny. Two brothers were now at logger heads—a family at war.

My mum and May wanted to pull off the common and shift but fair play to Jim, he refused as did my dad. They hadn't started the fight Jessie had, so let it be him who shifted but we knew how stubborn Jessie was so he wouldn't shift either.

Both brothers looked a sight, black yocks, bumps and bruises was shared by both, not a pretty sight and full of hate for each other right now. But you can bet your last shilling if any man challenged either of them out to fight the other would run to his aid—that's how it works in all families, they can beat each other to a pulp but no one else is allowed to.

My dear mum was upset and for once, my dad agreed with her. His old mum was at the bottom of this and so agreed May and Jim.

"I've never hit an old woman my Len, but if she starts on me, I'll take a crack at her, it won't become me, I know that, but I promise you I'll take my crack at her."

Jim told my dad that when they got to the lane they should pull on to the green in front the Prince of Wales public house and walk back to check on the old couple—that was agreed by both brothers as the best thing to do—that way me mam and the old granny would not come face to face.

And so a few days later, we left Bath behind us and took the road, which is a hard old drag on our horses to the Prince lane. On leaving the outskirts of Bath, the road drops steeply down to Dunkerton then steeply up towards Peas down St John. Hard work even for our fit horses pulling and holding back heavy wagons up and down two such steep hills and we all had to vacate the wagon and walk the few miles on foot till we reached the stopping place by passing the bottom entrance of the lane.

Where we pulled right outside the pub on the green, it was like a mini common with the pub on one side and the main road on the other, but it also had the top entrance to the Prince lane situated on it. It was, I believe, council land back in those days, but now it is part and parcel of the old public house as a garden.

As far as we children were concerned, it was not a good place to stop on. We were warned not to play near the road. We were strictly ordered not to play in front of the pub. Well that left only the entrance to the lane which we was told to keep out of, which left us to sit round the yog and that never suited us older ones at all.

And so Jim and my dad left to visit the old granny and granddad. We knew some of his other brothers was pulled up the lane because from the top of Dunkerton hill, the lane came into plain view in winter when the trees and hedges was bare of the leaves. That's how we saw the wagons and raising smoke from the yogs—that meant the old ones had plenty of company.

There was Jim said a bit of to do, when they got down the lane. At the sight of my dad, they knew he had been fighting and my dad told them who he had fought and why and asked where his mum was because she had not showed herself.

She had gone up the village shop with two of my dad's sister –in-laws to fetch shopping he was told. Not the best news for Jim and my dad to hear, knowing fully well the shoppers would have to pass by my mum to get back down the lane.

The family was split on the rows between my dad and cripple Jessie. Granddad was upset that two of his sons had fought each other and it was down to his old Emma. She was the cause of all this, and he was going to tell her so. In no uncertain terms, the old granny was in for ructions when she got back. He hated his family falling out with each other but by letting his old woman take the reins a few years back, on family issues because of his failing health, he had set the cat among the pigeons. Now he had had his fill of family rows and bickering, there was more trouble brewing on the old granny's return.

"Back up the lane," as we sat round the yog, poor aunt May said uneasily to my mum, "my Vie just dick up the tober, tis the old woman with two others coming down to the lane."

My mum was up and on her toes in seconds.

"You keep back, my May, and make sure the other two don't interfere."

Me and our Alfie stood behind my mum—fret on to death at what my mum would do to the old granny.

"Our Alfie," I whispered, "run like lightening down and fetch my dad afore my mum mourns the old granny."

"Shan't," he said, "you go. I'm staying with my mum."

"I shan't leave my mum either," I told him.

By now we could see it was aunt Kizzie, Tom's wife, and Leal, Dan's woman, with the old granny. We knew Kizzie would not get involved, but was not so sure about Leal, a stocky well-built woman, a bit of a pet of the old granny.

"If she lays a finger on my mum, I'll kick her in the shins," our Alfie said, when I told aunt May to watch Leal.

"And we'll help," piped up Lilea and Jimmy.

"They ain't gonna hurt my Aunt Fiance," cried Jimmy.

The old granny had a bit of a surprise on seeing my mam. She knew Jim's wagon, but had not known our wagon, because she had not set yocks on it before.

As the three drew level with the pub, out walked my mum to meet them. They stopped dead in their tracks at the sight of this little woman who looked up for it. Chest stuck out, my mum said, "It's me and you, old woman, and if these two interfere, I'll set about them as well, strike me stone dead, if I don't set about the three on you if they two step in."

"You wouldn't hit an old woman?" asked Leal all mealy mouthed, because she knew my mum meant business this morning.

"That nasty old bitch been and got my Lenard and cripple Jessie fighting," answered my mum.

"Two of your sons fighting over you, you bloody old cow, are you satisfied now you have broken up the family and got two brothers trying to mour each other—a fine mother you turned out to be—and no Leal, I would and will hit an old woman—she that old maggoty face bastard have made my life a misery for years, it ends here today—all because she ain't seen her son for a few months. Well I'll tell yous this, I ain't seen my family in years, but my family don't fight over me—they're better than that old bastard there," pointing at the old granny.

Then the old woman let fly.

"You, you little black-headed Devonshire painted whore dolly—you been causing trouble in this family since the day my boy had you. Get back down Devonshire with your gorgie family—where you belong."

"Gorgie is it old woman? I'll tell you this much, my family is more traveller than you'll ever be and better people than you'll ever be. You should have died at birth like you squatted poor little Iky when you laid on him and squatted him to death, you wicked old mare!"

The old woman pulled out ready to land my mum one fist up in the air.

"I'll tell you this old woman, I'll give you the first hit, but make it a good one for I'm going to rip you from limb to limb."

But before my mum had a chance to carry out her threat, my dad, Jim, Tom, Dan and Joe had rushed in between them—Joe had his arms around my mum.

"No, my Fiance, don't hit her, she'll get you locked up," then he turned on his mum.

"My dad's waiting on you—you best get down the lane and face the music old gal."

With all the noise going on, it fetched the drinkers out the pub and the landlord—they stood with glasses in their hands expecting to see a bit of sport and were duly threatened to get back inside or get a hiding. They took the easy way and went inside.

Joe, Jim and Tom were forcing the three women back down the lane.

It was Jim on his return who told us how the old granddad had beat the old woman. He had not set about her in years, but told her it was overdue. She had took too much for her own way, now it was over. He sent a message back to my mum and dad to tell them they could pull in the lane any time they wanted and for as long as they wanted the same as the rest of his family—and would be welcome.

Although my dad would go back many times to visit his parents, my mum never would and he could never coax her in going, till granddad passed away many years later as then she did go back, but never spoke to the old woman. That is until it was the old granny's time to part from this world and my mum was called up on by the family to see to her. The old woman had a growth which broke out in her side, as the others would not wash and dress the wound, the nurse showed my mum what to do and fair play to my mum as she told me later in life, she had lit her candle to the devil.

It's not very nice when one of our families has a big fall out, because travelling as we all do, we could meet the family members who are at logger heads anywhere in our area—and old grudges die hard.

But May and Jim, Joe and Ally were very loyal to my mum and dad while at the same time on the best of terms with the rest of the family.

It was not until 1950 that all the family mended their fences and became a whole family again. That was the year we lost our Little Jess—a very tragic episode in our lives, I have recorded it in *Our Forgotten Years.*

There was no winter farm work for us this year. When our wagons was packed and ready for the road, Joe known as 'Cock Eyed Joe' and Ally came up the lane with their wagon to join us for the winter months.

Now there were three brothers all travelling together—all good compatible company, the men would work together as would the three women.

We ended up pulled on the lanes above Shepton Mallet, high up on the Mendips—a cold bitter place in winter; tis said they got two winters in one up on the Mendips—but our men knew the lanes and where to pull in a spot that would give us a bit of shelter for the coming bad weather. High hedges afforded shelter from the winds and gave us plenty of wood for the yog. All three families would now be sharing the one yog, with the wagons pulled in a half circle facing the yog—much like the wagons did in Indian raids in the cowboy films we would walk miles to see at times.

The men would torment my mum on how she went for their old mum.

"She would have ate you if she got a hold on you," Jim would say. "She's twice the size of you little un."

Then Joe would laugh and say, "Well, my money would have been on that little terrier."

Then my dad would laugh and say, "I wouldn't have liked to see it happen, but my Vie would have took my mum's lips off."

My mum, being who she was took it all in good part—she liked these two brothers of my dad, and could see no harm in them. And me and our Alfie loved their children. We were more like brothers and sisters than cousins. Jim was the apple of me eye with Joe coming a close second in my favourite uncles.

The men cut loads of Elder sticks to make the huge wooden chrysanthemum flower heads. They would sit round the yog for hours on end, chatting away while they worked being very careful not to let any of the Elder get in the yog, that was known to bring bad luck down on us.

The Romani Gypsies are a very superstitious race of people—crossed knives-elder and ivy in the yog—three animals, if their names are mentioned, means bad luck. Their names begin with 'M', 'R' and 'S', I can't even bring myself to write their names—if a superstition has been passed on down through the past generations its cemented in our way of life, in fact our very life style is partly governed by such superstitions.

Of course we learn of all the superstitions from very young, so they are embedded in our minds and memory, and that's how they get passed on from generation to generation.

It was lovely to sit round the old smoky yog watching the flower heads fall or chucked on to the sheet provided for the purpose of not getting them dirty or muddy in any way. When they have dried out a bit, the women would put colour dyes on them, rich red-yellow or pink, the dye would be made from off cuts of the different coloured crepe paper used in the making of wax roses and kept by just for this purpose.

This is a wonderful life even in the winter months, life sat round the yog while everyone was busy doing their own thing. The smells from the frying pans or the old black pots simmering away pushed into the red hot embers soon made you realise how hungry you were. These for me were some of the best times, a family gathering you might say.

Christmas was now just round the corner—the men went out and bought a tidy four wheeled trolly, to make everyone's life that much easier. The women could drive it to fetch shopping either to Shepton Mallet or Midsomer Norton or Radstock, it was a wide choice for them in such a hilly part of this county.

The men would use it to cut and fetch Holly and Mistletoe. The Holly was for wreath making—wreath hoops-wires were bought and stored ready to be mossed up, moss picked out of banks and woods were bagged up and put by ready for use.

Christmas to us lot was more of a gorgie holiday for them, and a money making time for us lot. It never meant that much to us in these early days—yes—we chavvies would hang up our socks on bushes or where ever we found somewhere to hang them. And we four older ones moved ours that often to make sure the old Father Christmas mush could easily find them. This was serious business for four excited young ones so they had to be hung where they could easily be spotted by the night time visitor.

Even the prickly job of Holly wreath making was enjoyable for us lot. Although classed as women's work with their nimble fingers, the men would do little jobs such as breaking off the stems of Holly for the women to knit in to the moss bound hoop—the whole lot of us had a hand in this Christmas work.

There was no need to tramp round the shops taking orders for them in advance, these wreaths once seen by the shopkeepers would sell themselves.

Most shops would take a dozen or so wreaths and a few bunches of the wooden brightly coloured chrysanthemums to put on display outside their shops—the towns folks and villagers would snap them up for their loved ones grave or to hang on their doors and in these old days they knew they was lucky to get them, because it was mostly only the Gypsies who made and supplied them. So at least we got a Christmas welcome in to the areas we stopped in at this time of the year, and the local community near to where we had pulled in would come to the wagons to buy our Christmas trading goods. Some bearing gifts of spuds or a cabbage. Even a bit of fresh meat or chicken from the farmers and stop to chat awhile with us. Some knew our families because this is a very old stopping area so they have got to know us over the past years and a few would even know our first names—that was real nice.

We got the usual visit from the Shepton Mallet police who told us to leave the place clean and tidy when we left. This was an insult in itself—for the only trace we would leave behind is where we lit the yog and where the horses while on plug chains had cropped circles of grass right to the ground. To leave a place with as little trace of us as possible is yet one more of the Gypsy travelling strict rules because we return again and again to our stopping places. This practice is done by all Gypsies country wide. We leave it as near as damb it in a perfect order—the fires are inspected time again to make sure they are out and not left burning on the roadside. It is against the law, police law and a heavy fine if caught doing so.

So it was a veiled dig at our men folk, because the police had been told by shopkeepers and others that our Christmas work was a bonus for them. And if we was shifted on that bonus would be lost but our men never made any thing of it. It would be pointless any way to fall out with them for after Christmas weather permitting we would be long gone of our own accord to pastures new.

Then come Christmas Eve, the money made on the Holly wreaths had been shared three ways. All three men had got a surprise because they never knew how many wreaths had been made and sold so was happy with the seasons work as was the women. All the holly rubbish had been burnt but the thick sticks had been put aside to cook the Christmas dinner on. On the morrow our yog and roast goose would smell delightful from being cooked over a holly and apple wood. The apple wood from the branches the mistletoe grew on, not only round our camp but up and down the old road. This would be our yearly special yog enjoyed by all.

Since we got up out of our beds on the morning, we chavvies were looking for the likely spot to hang or hitch our socks to-and getting into trouble with the parents. The most troublesome ones being myself and Joe and Ally's Cathy. Cathy was born mostly blind, she could just see shadows, but could get about well enough. She had adjusted her sight to living on the roads, mind you the poor cow had no choice, and sing, she never stopped singing. She could be a spoilt pest at times—her parents had spoiled her rotten so she had me running round finding her the best place to hang her sock. We found that many best spots, only for her to change her mind a few minutes later, her sock nearly ended up on the yog I can tell you, but after my mum threatened to take me lips off, for upsetting poor little Cathy, my uncle cock-eyed Joe took over. Finding that bestest place to hang the sock till he got tired of following his sweet little lamb about. Of all the places her sock ended up tied to the handle of her pram, which she pushed in between the sharves of their wagon. Cathy was about twelve or fourteen at this time of her life—she was a lot older than the rest of us and the pram which Aunt Ally used to push her in while out calling and a pretty sight it was too. Cathy was a well-built gal and quite tall for her age. Now picture her sitting in a pram with her legs hanging over the bottom of it, singing like a nightingale with a sore throat. She was a case alright.

My mum told May and Ally, "I'll be glad when nightfall comes, they chavvies is driving me mad."

"Leave the poor little buggers be, my Vie," answered my dad after over-hearing what she had said. "They are excited."

"Then you men take the lot of um and fetch wood and water—tire the lot right out."

"Tis our Maggie making trouble," shouts our Alfie.

"Now hark at that little mush—trying to get me in more trouble, as if I was not in enough already. Just you wait, I told him, till I gets you round that corner. I'll make you squeal for your mum—you just wait and see if I don't,"

"That's it Lenard," she shouted. "Take these chavvies away before I mours the lot of um."

And so my dad Jim and Joe rounded us all up. With Joe pushing Cathy, who was sitting lopsided in the pram up along the road collecting stumps of wood, thick stumps that would not burn away too quick.

That's when me and our Alfie got at it. One of the biggest mistakes, that brother of mine made, was to teach me how to fight. How to stand and throw my weight with a punch and how to make a proper fighting fist. So I was a good match for him, if I got the first punch in that was. If not, he would floor me so I made sure he never seen my first punch coming. Then it was all shouting as we tangled and fought. It was Jim who grabbed our Alfie and shooked him—telling him off for fighting with his poor little sister—not knowing I started it. And I was not going to own up that I did so we both got ourselves in hot water with my dad.

"No grub for you two today, you can starve for all I care," my dad threatened us.

"Now pick up that wood, take it back to the wagons and come right back—I'll punish you one way or another."

To make matters worse Jimmy and Lilea were falling about laughing at our downfall.

"Just you wait," we both told them, "just you wait, now we." Two friends turning on the other three for our Robert was now joining in on their side—with that Cathy singing at the top of her voice about the singing policemen.

I could have just easily ripped her lips off, my God, when I think of how me and that dear brother of mine fought each other as kids. It's a wonder we never moured each other.

Come nightfall, none of us could sleep. We were so excited and worked up as to what that old Father Christmas mush would leave for us. While the grownups sat round the outside yog and talked of Christmas's past—our wagons being as warm as toast with the little queenie stoves going, to keep us warm each night.

Christmas morning—we woke up to a crispy hard frost, and on poking our heads out the wagon spied a roaring yog. My dad had been up and made a huge yog as he did every morning, but this morning it seemed bigger and brighter than normal. Don't know what time we woke up, as time meant little to us back in those days. As we rushed from the wagon squealing in delight, my dad was saying, "Come on my babies have a kushti."

"Warm, morning dad, morning mum," we all cried out.

"Did the mush come then," we asked. "Did he find us then, that old Father Christmas mush?"

"Yes," answered my mam.

"He came so get yourselves sat down."

My dad and Jim had spread a canvas sheet round most sides of the yog and the heat from the yog had warmed it up so as we squatted down round the yog. It was cosy and warm. Mind you, we all had our jackets on, as we did on cold winter mornings. Then we were handed our socks just as Jimmy and Lilea came running out their wagon—nuts, apples and a few sweets were found in our socks, and besides that we all had a knitted sort of stocking filled with little miniature toys. This was grand. It was a fine Christmas morning and on top of this we each were given a bundle of rolled up second hand clothes-jackets and jumpers. Our mums had bought and begged, and hid away for this day. We were fit to burst with happiness because this was the only period in our lives that magic entered it. These early Christmases held that bit of magic when we chavvies believed in that old father Christmas mush—and we so appreciated every little thing we were given—and looked after it like grim death.

Although we all liked balls, we were not allowed them. Balls had been the death of a child years afore we were born. He had been playing with a ball and ran after it without looking right in front of an army lorry and died. So most of the families had banned the playing with balls as our roadside stopping places were no place for balls.

When Joe brought Cathy to the yog, she was clutching a beautiful dolly. How me and our Lilea envied that dolly, wishing we had one to play with. But Cathy knew and let us both play with it later in the day, and she could play with our presents. We all knew not to take toys which belonged to others without asking but on the other hand would be given a "yes, yis can play with it" from its young owner, when asked.

The big black iron pots belonging to three families were being filled with water and pushed in to the hot embers to come to the boil, which may take up to an hour. So dinner cooking was a long drawn out job each day.

My mum having fed us our breakfast of boiled eggs and hot toast, which had been toasted over the embers by a clean cut thin stick pushed through the crust and then toasted, was busy getting her goose washed and stuffed, ready to roast in her biggest pot, which would also roast some spuds and onions at the same time. Her roasting pot was pushed in the embers to heat up with a drop of water in it and an enamel plate laid face down in the bottom of the pot. This would stop the roasting meat from sticking to the bottom of the pot. Once the meat was put in, it would be surrounded with spuds and onions and a parsnip or two. So that as it slowly roasted each would flavour the other things in the pot—this would be a meal fit for the king, or so my uncle Joe had said.

Later we heard the farmer coming up the lane on his old tractor to feed his heard of cows. The milking cows had been milked hours since, now he was to feed his younger stock. We got on well with this farmer and he never minded us stopping near his land, in fact he had told our men folk to help themselves to clean water from his cow trough—minding to always shut the gate. For the road we were pulled on led past a stone quarry and big lorries would whizz fast up and down it as we all was well aware of.

"Morning!" he shouted above his engine noise. "Merry Christmas to you all," and got down off the tractor and produced a big wooden crate. "Here you are," he laughed, "a Christmas present from me and my wife."

Jim took the box and every one thanked him and said to thank his wife.

"Must get on," he said, "cattle needs feeding, oh and yes you can fetch another bale of hay for your horses later this morning" and off he went, he had been selling our men hay for our horses ever since we pulled in.

On emptying the crate they found that the dear woman had put three of everything in the crate for the three families. Three small Christmas cakes homemade, cheese, butter and homemade sweets for us lot. The farmer had added cabbages, carrots and other vegetables. It was a most welcome Christmas gift for us all.

"You see there are kind folks out there. God bless that mush," said Ally, in her old fashioned way of talking.

Then from beside the yog we heard Cathy shouting at Lilea, "Don't, don't you Lilea—give me back my dolly."

"Oh dear, that Lilea." Cathy had given her the dolly to hold and look at and in a flash Lilea, being nosey like myself, had half undressed it to see what it had on underneath the dress, and poor Cathy was now crying as loud as a bull bellowing, "mum my dolly, mum my dolly."

Thinking she was being murdered, we all turned to the yog, sure enough Lilea was busy undressing the dolly, taking no heed of Cathy's crying.

Aunt May, bless her, took the doll off Lilea at the same time giving her a good clip round her ear. While the others tried to calm down Cathy, but Cathy was on a mission. She had been wronged and was going to make the most of it. Her bellowing continued loud and clear, Lilea, she now bellowed had broken her dolly.

"Come here my baby gal," soothed my mum.

"I'll mend your dolly. Hush up crying and come by aunt Vie," as she gently pulled Cathy to her feet and sat her down close by her. But Cathy was upset and when Cathy was upset, she let king and country know it. Her bellowing got louder while my mam fumbled to put the little dress and shoes back on the dolly.

"You bad gal," uncle Jim told Lilea.

"She told me to do it," she said pointing right at me which now put me in the lime light of all their anger.

"I never did our Lilea."

"You are a great big lying cow, I never did tell you to take the dolly's clothes off," and then shock my ear. It was stinging as if I got stung by a bunch of stinging nettles. My mam had clipped my ear for me. Me as innocent as a new babe, well not quite, for I had told Lilea earlier I wondered what the doll had on under the dress, but never told her to undress it. "Oh that Lilea is a bad gal."

My punishment was to peel the spuds, carrots and parsnips and washing them good and clean. I was not a happy gal that Christmas morning after all. Even my dad chastised me for egging Lilea on and that gal surely to God never needed any egging on. After I had done what I had been told to do, my mum came to check I had done it right, and I whispered, "I never did tell Lilea to do that my mum."

"I knows you never," she answered.

"But why did you have to hit me then?"

"To keep the peace," she said.

On this day of all days, peace must be kept, and me, I was punished for something my mum knew I had not done in the first place, just to keep the peace. I just don't understand the grownups one bit.

Then to the surprise of one and all this big car pulled up and a real lady got out.

"Merry Christmas," she said. "Here's a little gift for your beautiful children—from the ladies of the village."

"Thank you, kindly mum," said May taking the big cardboard box.

"Thank you kindly and a very merry Christmas to you all."

"Well, have a lovely day and remember it's our Lord's birthday today or something like that," she had said and left.

I can still smile to myself when I think of the emptying of that box, like the farmer's gift. We thought it might hold cakes and sweets. What it held was lots of pairs of mittens and scarves made up of it seemed dozens of different colours of knitting wool, pull-on woolly hats, three Christmas puddings and a pile of religious leaflets and not one of us could read a word to save our lives.

"But it was the thought that counts," said my mum.

"And you lot will look lovely in these hats and gloves." This comment upset our Alfie and Jimmy.

"We shan't wear that," they hollered. "That's gals' things." Their pride had suffered a blow—to think they would have to wear such colourful things.

But it had brought some cheer into a beautiful cold frosty day and the thought of the old ladies spending hours knitting up the things for us made us happy. They were good Christian folks.

Our dinner turned out handsome—and the sneaky three men had several bottles of old brown ale, and bottles of ginger ale for us chavvies hid away, which they brought out and shared to go with our dinner. So yes, Cock eyed Joe was right when he said our dinners were fit for a king—and the smell from the holly and apple wood burning on our yog still lingered about the place. All in all, it was a grand day to store in our memory boxes—which we all did.

Boxing Day was the day the men would go to the nearest pub and come back singing their heads off. While more cooking got done by the women—and we chavvies played our own games of climbing trees to swinging on farmer's gates, running back every so often for a warm by the yog and a bit to eat or drink.

All too soon we were in a New Year and back to our travelling ways. It was decided by all that we would give the wild flowers a miss and take our time travelling down country to Blandford in Dorset. We had been there before a few times, and now we would be dropping the rag bills around the doors—so having the trolly was just the thing for this kind of work. Rags and woollens we had heard were making a fair price so be it. It was back on the old door-knocking job.

Although we had had a kushti happy Christmas and New Year, we were not too sad to leave the Mendips and get down on to lower country. It had been a bitter cold stay above Shepton Mallet—so now we would head for that well known area of Yeovil. Then on to the Dorset boarder which was well known to our parents. We were in no rush so the men made wooden pegs and me and Lilea was collared to go out daily hawking the villages with our mams as we came to them. The dads would look after the children left in their care till we got back later in the afternoons. Naturally me and our Lilea were split up and hawked opposite sides of the street for they knew we two hawking the same side could mean trouble. We were as bad as each other for falling in and out but we were never ever cheeky to the folks who opened their doors to us—that really would have brought trouble and disgrace down on us both and a goodly clip round our ears. We had been brought up to ignore the house dwellers who could be pretty rude on answering their door to find one of us on their doorstep. It had been drummed in to us all not to answer back our elders—whoever they may be, and we did on the whole abide by this. But at times, little words would just sort of slip out the corner of our mouths—a mouth that was a full time job keeping shut.

But on these cold days you never heard any two gals grumble like we two did. "I'm cold, I want to pee, I'm hungry." On and on we went, till we were told in no uncertain terms our dads would be told how bad we had behaved. When we got back to the wagons this shut us up for a while but not for long, and our mums kept a strict eye on us especially if we were chatting to a house dweller for too long on their doorstep. They would make it their business to come and check out what was going on and put us on our way. Of course me and Lilea were not told of the danger one can came across, when knocking on doors. No one explained what kind of danger we could find ourselves in and we never found out till we had grown up.

That there are a few really bad men and women in this world, who would get a child in their house and make them do bad dirty things, or young women too, if they could.

We never had a clue of such things as well our parents knew that's why a tight rein was put on us gals when out calling and when on fetching wood and water we were made to go in groups, on the pretext of all fetching some of whatever we were fetching. It was a safety thing for our own safety.

When we were old enough to be told such things, we learned that over the years some of our women had been assaulted and badly frightened while out hawking.

Thinking back on it all now, to rear a young family back then must have been one big worry on the parents. There was so much danger in our everyday lives. They were kept on their toes keeping us safe and sound from road traffic, to ponds and rivers, and horse accidents to the fear of a bad person lurking behind a closed door awaiting such children as us lot. My God, tis a wonder we all survived thinking back on it, and they were so right to worry for did we not lose our Little Jess in a horse related accident. A dear little seven-year-old boy, our dear younger brother—I recorded his death in *Our Forgotten Years* with photos of his funeral. Our little Jess was one of many young Gypsy children to be killed in accidents when parents were travelling the roads. Some were horse-related, others by getting too close to the yog catching their clothes on fire. Some got knocked down with traffic and some drowned in rivers. When young, you don't see the dangers our parents could see.

We chavvies had a wonderful care-free childhood but it was only the love and care and worry by our parents that made it. So no, we never had brand new fancy bikes or dolls' prams simply because we could not carry them outside the wagons. But what we did have was open common land, green lanes and side roads to play on—fields full of dandelions, buttercups, cowslips and wood's full of the strong sweet smelling bluebells to run and play free as the wild birds, everything nature had or grew was free to us. We lacked neither food nor drink or warmth and there's not many communities who can say that. We took for granted what nature offered, and used it to make saleable crafts or use the wild flowers to earn part of our living. We were not taking bread out of anyone else's mouths we earned our own.

But now we had been travelling for about a month or more and reached the Shaftesbury common land. What a beautiful long stretched out common this was and I must say there was a few really lovely old fashioned families already stopping on it. A few wagons and tents were scattered here and there, all old Dorset families who very rarely left the Dorset area. But was well known to us or I should say the grown-ups of our little group.

Not being too used to this common, the first thing I noticed was the herby smell of it. When walking on the grass you crushed the herbs growing under foot and the smell wafted upwards. It was so different and grand, it wasn't like some of the commons round Wellington, in Somerset that was mired in wild heather. This common was made up of many different herby grasses and plants and it showed in the horses belonging to the travellers pulled on there. For their coats was thick and shiny, although our horses was in good condition they made ours look like poor relations but a few weeks here would change all that.

Everyone was shaking hands in greeting each other and were glad to see new faces and to hear each other's news and a bit of gossip on the side.

And we found their chavvies exciting and good fun to play with. Of course every one made a fuss of poor Cathy—that's how they talked of her, poor little Cathy. She wasn't poor or so little I thought to myself. She could make three of me, me being short in the legs and as thin as a razor blade, but still it was always sad to think she could not see much of what we could see in our everyday life.

These families were the Maidments, Barnys, Benhamsand Turners—great lot of people. I so enjoyed our longish stay among them.

These Dorsett Travellers made a different living to what we did. They hawked out baskets made of rushes and rush mates brushes of all sizes-combs, boot laces and other little much needed home made things and some of the men were knife grinders, and thatch roof stakes. All manner of skills these people possessed, very old skills it was lovely to see the things they made to sell—so different from ours.

After settling in, our men went out dropping their rag bills then picked them up again the next day. They brought back all manner of things because there was very few families collecting rags down this part of the country in those days.

When it came time of an evening to sort and bag the rags it was good to see our men letting the other common dwellers, pick out good clean coats, jackets and whatever out of their rags; it was a time to share.

Share a like—we had our laughs too. When one or the other tried to force themselves in a jacket that was far too small for them, or a woman getting into a frock that swamped her body, yes those were good days. But after a few weeks, our men had run out of local places to go, so it was shifting to a new area where we would start all over again—rags got weighed in. More sack bags bought or borrowed—hesin bags were a tool of the trade.

Saying farewell was quite sad for these families we were about to leave had been good company and old friendships had been re-cemented once again. Yes, we would miss their company.

We never wanted to leave this common and its old-fashioned travellers but were forced to for want of new places to drop our rag bills. Our men had to work each and every day, except Sundays, and if the men never went out the women would; hawking their flowers or clothes pegs—that's how it was back then.

This is a lovely part of the country, a bit out of our own area, but no one minded that at all, for the Dorset bred Gypsies would at times take a wander over in to other areas, such as to Bridgwater to pick the beans and peas—and got the same kind of welcome as they had given our little group. Gypsies countrywide accepted this and welcomed the straying families—a code of conduct, you might say, in today's society.

After pulling out we headed for Blandford forum—taking weeks as we dropped rag bills in all the little villages on route and us chavvies seeing and enjoying new places. With the grownups always looking for stopping places with wind shelter, March could be a very cruel month. With bitter high winds and our wagons could easily get blown over, double worry was that with the little iron queenie stoves going meant if it tipped over, it would catch on fire and all could be lost. This had happened in families more than a few times so our stopping places had to be picked with care for our own safety and that of our belongings.

The villages we passed through looked prettier than the ones in Somerset or so I thought. But maybe it was because I had not seen them before and the house dwellers knew we were strangers in their area. And some we knew reported us to the local police station who would come to our stopping places and check us out, asking to see our hawking licenses–which was duly shown, and where in the country we had come from. They noted everything our men said and recorded it down in little books. They were pretty strict with their questions and demanded answers but easier on shifting us on by not demanding we pack up and shift there and then. But warned us that they would be keeping an eye on our movements.

"The gavers must fly with the rooks," laughed cock eye Joe, "if they can keep a yock on us lot." Which brought a few remarks and laughs from the rest of us. When we did shift a few miles on and he spotted a rook, he would holler, "Hey up, gavers about," pointing at the flying birds. He was a right old case cock eye Joe.

And so our travels took us slowly on through Blandford—back around on to the old Dorchester road. We were travelling in a huge big circle and dropping rag bills or hawking the doors all the way. March had turned into April, with the weather getting kinder by the week. By the beginning of May we were on our side of Dorchester but it was decided to try all the out laying villages before we hit the Yeovil road and made for our own area. We had nothing to rush back for, as our time was our own.

This could take weeks or months it was a good time in our lives. All three families were happy and enjoyed each other's company. They found a quiet lane, and all three men set about painting and tidying up their wagons and spent hours rubbing down and grooming their horses, till they shined like glass bottles. First they washed them in a lovely clear running brook, which our horses seemed to enjoy. Then using handfuls of rough grass set about their coats. With the women seeing to their cooking pots making a meal—those were carefree days, warm weather and every one in good health and spirits—we must have made a pretty picture against a background of lush green fields and hedges.

After the men had finished doing their spring cleaning on the outside of the wagons, it was then the women's turn—all bedding was hung out to air. The queenie stove now not in so much use was wiped down and black-leaded. Then out came the scrubbing brushes, floors and all the wooden bits in the wagons was scrubbed with carbolic soap suds and then wax polished with the thick mansion polish bought in a round tin, which smelled of lavender. These women and men like all Gypsies were cock proud of their horses and little home on wheels so looked after both with pride.

We would miss the pea picking season this year but it made no matter, our little families was doing well for themselves— at their own pace—as we heard the grownups discuss as we all sat round our yog on a peaceful evening.

"Wonder how the old couple is," said Jim.

"When we get back, I'll take a dander on my hoss up to visit them."

This was a subject he knew had to be brought up for very little had been said over the past months of the other half of the family. Jim, as they say, had broken the ice. The three brothers were very loyal to each other but also at the same time were loyal to their parents no matter what had happened in the past and would go through hell and high water to visit them, and give help if needed.

"Yes, I was wondering how my dad was faring," said my dad.

"I'll come with you our Jim and count me in," laughed cockeye Joe.

My mum knew this had to be done so kept her comments to herself and there was old Tom to think of. My dad's eldest brother who was not so well in health—the brothers Alfie, John and Dan and Jessie could fend for themselves. But Tom may need a quiet hand shake to help him out because his working days were over. He only had his woman Kizzie to go out hawking to keep him and their children, so a little collection would be made and handed to Tom on the quiet—hence it's known as a 'quiet hand shake.'

And by doing this old custom in the quiet, Tom's pride wouldn't get dented in any way. This is how they would give the collection to Tom, when they visited the folks down the Prince Lane, one of them would wait and pick their moment and would sit next to Tom and when the others were occupied with their chatting or dealing, a hand would slip in Tom's jacket pocket. A poke in the ribs from inside the pocket would make Tom aware that he had been given a quiet handshake. This done, they could leave feeling happy that they had given their brother a much needed leg up and his thank you would be a tear in his dear old yocks as he bid them farewell.

There was no bragging on any one's part when these handshakes were given. It was done and hidden to save the pride of the person it was given to. It happens quite often in families, with the loss of a loved one who passed away or on the loss of an only driving horse or wagon. Collections could be made at the drop of a hat passed to the one in need and never mentioned again. That's Gypsy ways—a very caring way and given with a good heart.

But we were not done with hawking and billing these pretty little villages yet. I loved the evening when the three men would make dozens of grosses of clothe pegs after going off cutting their hazel sticks. They would sit round the yog working like a conveyer belt—one would strip the outer skin off the sticks and cut them to length on the old molly block. While the next man would tin the pegs by putting a narrow band of tin round one end of the peg to stop it splitting when in use on the clothe lines, and the third man would finish the peg by mouthing it, cutting a vee shape which would grip the clothes to the line and the women would 'train up' the pegs by threading three dozen on to a thin strip of hazel stick. Then the finished pegs would be put aside to dry out. When freshly made afore they dried, these pegs had a lovely smell of the young green hazel wood, and still had a whiff of the smell when they reached the house dwellers doors, a family affair one might say.

When pulled on high ground one day, the sea was pointed out to us group of chavvies. In the distance was a blue-green sea, it seemed to reach the sky. Our Alfie and the rest was begging to be taken down to it, but not me. I did not like the look of such a big span of deep water as I feared it. No, the rest could do what they liked but leave me out of it, and I've had a fear of water all my life. It's never left me—I really don't know why, but I do fear deep water.

Anyway, it was too far to drive to from where we were pulled in. My dad told them so they never got to see the sea which made this one very happy.

After a few more weeks of every one pulling their weight working together, we hit the old Yeovil road. Although it was a kushti change to be out of our own area for a few months, there was a feeling of excitement that we were heading back to our own well-known stopping places of friends and family. It was now summer time—hedges in full bloom. Every bank and hedgerow was smothered in primroses, violets and buttercups, cow parsley and all the normal herbs and flowers, it made a pretty picture. I think all my life I had a love affair with old Mother Nature and still have to this day. Every plant and tree held its own beauty for me—pretty perfumed ones, stinky wild garlic ones, ugly ones; they were a part of my travelling days. I really loved and enjoyed it, as well as the wild life that came with it. We knew every wild animal, insect and birds as they too were part of and shared our life style. I confess I truly loved my travelling days, come rain, hail or snow whatever nature chucked at us, it was taken as it was and with the comfort of good parents we young ones had it all. Everything we played with was free and given by nature with each season of the year. If you were lucky enough to be born in to a Romani Gypsy family and brought up in the old ways on the road, you were a very rich person indeed and the fact that you had the knowledge of the wild life around.

You and each plant that grew only had a few short weeks to bloom. Make their seeds afore dying back in to the ground till the next season—that's mother nature for you.

In parts, it was a long old drag up hills to reach the town of Yeovil—so we would pull in after just a few miles to give our horses an afternoon and night's rest. Because we always tried to pull back out on the road in the morning part of the day—in winter it would warm up our horses and in the hot summer it would be that much cooler for them—to pull their heavy load. So in the summer, we always tried to be pulled in off the highways by noon of the day. It just goes to show how organised our way of life was. Thinking ahead all the time, for the settled community had the idea we just wandered about willy nilly—but each move we made was fully discussed before we made that move—and we tried to avoid such villages where we knew from old that the village bobby was very strict on us stopping near his village. Thus, to avoid trouble we gave such places a wide berth.

On reaching the town of Yeovil—we pulled on the out skirts where the three mums could jump on a bus and go in to the well-known town to fetch a bit of shopping. They knew their run in this town and also knew the best shops to sell their pegs or barter for bacon and other things—whilst we back at the stopping place gathered wood and water while the men cared for their horses. Then, they would light the yog, which we younger ones were not allowed as yet to do. The only time we were handed a match was to light the candles on winter nights up in the wagon but had been trained hard and well before being allowed to even do this little job. Our parents were very careful and wary of letting us handle matches so we got to be responsible, young, half grown up chavvies—our lives depended on this rule. Moreover, our belongings, such as everything we owned were packed in that wagon—one mistake and it would be gone up in smoke—and we felt a little grown up by being able and trusted to light those candles. We were leaving our puppy stage behind us—under the mum and dad's good guidance that was. I had, like hundreds of others, worked the field working alongside them since I was three or four years old—peeled the spuds and other vegetables for nearly as long, but it was a step up to be handed one match and an empty match box and trusted to do a grown up job. Hence, their five chavvies were growing up, later there would be eight of us chavvies in our family group.

We could hardly wait for the mums to get back, neither could our dads. They needed their bit of baccy to roll a few fags. Most of the men smoked rollups and a lot of the elderly women smoked the clay pipes or just have a bit of a pipe sticking out the corner of their mouths. This looked a bit comical to me but they seemed to enjoy it.

At last, we saw the bus pull up and out came our three women carrying baskets of shopping. The greeting they got, one would think they'd been gone a week or more as we lot ran to meet them.

You might laugh in this day and age but a pig's cooked trotter was so welcome. As we sat round the yog nibbling at the small bones or a quarter of the little sprats each, we could stick thin long sticks in and roast on the yog, or my mum would fry them up for us. These were real treats for us for helping our parents—simple little things like that made us so happy. Sprats could only be had from a town out the fresh fish shops but the pigs trotters could be bought in most village butcher shops where they killed and cured their own meat and hot crusty bread was made in most village bake houses. So you could say eggs, milk, cheese and butter we bought at the farms, we lived very well. In those days, life was what you made it—you could sit on your ass and hope for handouts, such as the national assistance money paid out to underprivileged families in those days or live like we lived. Work your way round the country side—making and selling things or working the land. There was no end of jobs to be had, if you were willing to work, and looked for it, which by tradition we all did. No one could ever say that the Gypsies were work shy as we proved many times over that no job was too hard to do, so long as we were earning our bread and butter.

Sometimes, as we passed through villages or hawked the doors, we could hear some folks say,

"Oh look at those poor little children. They must be cold and hungry."

But you know and it is true that we lived much better than the folks making the remarks. Simply because of our way of life which gave us a bigger choice of shops, and the odd farmers wife sold or bartered food for pegs or flowers but they never knew of this and felt the Gypsy children were hungry and ill-treated—and worst of all that we were the underprivileged ones.

It may have looked by outsiders that we Gypsy children was treated hard and suffered but we never did. Yes, we lacked a school education but we had our own Romani education by working at our parents' side in all manner of work. Learning to cook, clean, ride a horse bare back and the boys learned all of their fathers' skills—this was education and it paid tenfold for it taught us not to be work shy and how to earn our living. This education stayed lifelong with all of us—at this period in our lives-the same as countless generations afore us. We could get by very well without reading or writing. We had no need of such knowledge, and at that stage in our travelling life style, whenever thought we ever would. This just goes to show how things can change in a few short years—for today, 2017, it would be a very difficult life without school education for many reasons.

From Yeovil, we took the road that would lead us back to Shepton Mallet, right back from where we had started out from. But it was summer not the bitter cold of winter and everything looked in a new light. Gone was the white frost coating trees and hedges. Now, one could see the shimmering of the midsummer heat as we slowly passed along. Smell the sweat from our horses as they put their heads down to pull the wagon up the hills. The sound of a loose shoe on one of our driving mares, pulling in so Jim could remove the fending shoe. Cut back the hard hoof and nail the shoe back on, which he and the others were expert at doing, job done we continued on our way—in a few days pulled on the same stopping place we had spent Christmas.

From our stopping place above Shepton Mallet, it was only a stone's throw from the village of Oakhill, where the men could branch off and take a short cut across the lanes to Radstock. And a couple of two or three miles up Bath hill to the Prince lane. So it was arranged, the three would drive the trolly on each ride bare back to check on the old folks. Come morning, you will notice once again the visit to check on the old folks was the men's first priority. It's one of our strongest customs. It just had to be done by our old Gypsy law, custom and ways. Nothing but death would have stopped these three brothers driving the miles that lay between us and the old folks from making that journey, it's family ties and loyalty.

Tom would also get his quiet handshake—to make his life a bit easier, brotherly love and tradition would come into play to an old fashioned family—as it did in all families back then. You may wonder why this old custom never meant my mum running back to visit her family, but the old rule in those days was that the wife would travel with her man's family, and would meet her own family on the roads as they travelled about. But my mum's family only travelled in Devonshire and my dad's family never travelled that far down but it didn't mean she never knew how her family was, because my mum and her sister Ellen would get gorgies to write letters to each other. And collect them from village post offices of their choice, which each other knew the address—as the saying goes "there's more than one way to skin a rabbit"—that's how they kept in touch.

The old farmer who had been good to us last Christmas stopped his tractor on sight of the wagons that was pulled in. He was pleased to see us, had a quick chat and went on his way.

Come morning, it was the trolly they chose to drive for their visit. So after a hurried breakfast went on their way—my dad looking a bit dubious as to the welcome he would get at the end of their journey, but that never stopped him going.

May and Ally decided to walk back down the hill to Shepton and fetch a bit of fresh bread and meat back while my mum had us lot to look after, including Cathy. She waved off her mum, then moments later started her crying, loud and clear, till Jimmy was sent to fetch the two women back, who had not got very far, to take Cathy in the pram with them.

"My Ally," said my mum, "Your gal's crying will bring the gavers on us. We'll all get locked up—when she starts there's no shutting her up. Please take her with you."

There was peace, perfect peace once Cathy had gone with her mum—but poor Ally would find it hard going pushing that gerth, heavy gal back up the steep hills. Cathy could walk as good as any of us, but was spoilt and lazy and loved being babied in the old pramulater. Her mum and dad were not strict enough with her and made a rod for their own backs. She could do hard work at times. Cathy lived a relatively full life, she could play all the rough games with us and get about on her own, nearly as good as we lot—but was spoilt from birth, and now her parents were paying the price for loving her too much and not letting her grow up as normal as possible. She was their baby and always would be.

While my mum boiled and washed our dirty clothes, she put me and Lilea to peel enough spuds to share between the three families. While the bigger boys fetched wood and water, she kept the smaller ones playing near the yog in her sights to make sure they never got near the road. It was all go for all of us doing our bits—hours and hours it seemed later Ally and May got back. Proper fagged out, they dropped to the ground. It must be all of a two mile uphill hard push for the two women taking turns pushing the pram full to the brim with Cathy back to the wagons and that Cathy singing her head off, so loud tis a wonder they never got heard way back to the town.

"You should have made that gal walk, my Ally. Just look at the state you are in. You is done yer self in my old gal."

"We tried," said May, "she wouldn't walk an inch—she's a bad gal ain't she Ally."

Oh dear Cathy heard these words and her singing turned into crying and her crying louder than her singing and that was bad enough.

"Push her under the hedge in the shade," said my mum, "and let her have it right out. She'll soon cry herself to sleep."

Soon my mum had said, half an hour later, she was still at it—enough to give a stone a headache, even the nearby birds left home.

It was early evening when the men returned. All looked happy enough from a distance—so the visit must have went well—and indeed on pulling in they said it was fine. The hot horse unhitched and tied up to cool down. It would get a bucket of fresh water after it did cool off—a hot horse and cold water can give it the colic—so it had to stand a while before being allowed to drink its fill.

There was good news and bad from the lane. The old granny had been sociable to her three sons. Jessie now stopping up the lane made friends with my dad but poor old Tom was coughing bad, real bad and spitting blood.

"Don't sound too kushti my Len," said my mum. "Did you slip him his handshake?"

"Yes, I did that and not one of um seen me do it. Which pleased the poor chap but we all worried about him my Vie. He ain't too kushti, the doctor mush is sending him up to Winsley." This was a TB hospital on top of a hill at Bath. Over the next couple of years, he made several stays in that hospital. I recorded his death in *Our Forgotten Years*.

But for now, we still had him with us. In his younger days, tis said he was a tall, well built, good-looking man—the eldest of the family. He had two wives and brought up two families. His first wife Jane died young, then he had Kizzie. I'm not too sure, but I think he had six children between the two women—or it could have been seven.

Chapter 6
Culture at its Best

But from my memory, I thought a great deal of him. He was, in my eyes, a grand man and all his family and friends thought the same.

Asking after the old granddad, we were told he still had the gout but was getting about quite well, and was so very pleased to see the return of his sons. He asked after my mum and us chavvies which we knew he would because he did care about us. He also asked if the three sons were coming back and pulling in the lane. On telling him he couldn't speak for the others, but my mam would never pull on the lane again.

"I thought that would be your answer, I don't hold no blame on her—you tell her that mind Lenard."

"I'll tell first chance I get," he told his dad.

My mum said she was sorry she might not see the old fella again but there would be no way she would go near that nasty old granny—well worse words than that, but I'm being nice for once.

There were not many more stubborn than my mum. She meant what she said, and it was useless trying to talk her out of it so my dad let it ride.

Soon the roads would be alive with many horses and wagons as the families made their drive back to other parts of the country from the pea fields. Thus it was decided that we shift on to Emborough Pond Lane's for that's the road a good few of them would travel, heading for Bath or Bristol and the Frome area. Some would travel through the towns and travel many days or weeks back to where they came from, but it would be good to pull in the lane where we could spend a few hours or days with all the different breeds of other travelling families—have a kushti old catch up.

That's how we ended back on a favourite old stopping place. My God if this lane could talk it could tell no amount of tales, and about the antics and capers of the old families. This has been a well-known stopping place for hundreds of years, also the police would turn a blind eye and leave the Gypsies in peace for a change, most of the time.

The first lot to turn up was 'Hard Times Joe' and his wife Janenett Bowers. 'Janenett'—pronounced as Jane-nett—and their growing family. It was quite a big family mostly young boys and twin gals. My dad and his brothers was very fond of Hard Times, as he was known, and they were cousins which in itself would have made them close to each other. We were well pleased to see them pull in.

Then came some of the Bristol Ayres family—the Loveridges, Smiths, Barnys, Benhems, Coopers, Lambs, you name them, they came. We had a great old time, until one family who I can't remember their name, only that the mother was called Rodie, pulled in. On greeting them, we were told their fourteen-year-old boy was bad up in the wagon—"He was bodily ill," the mother cried.

On going up and seeing him, the women chewed it over and told the boy's mum they should take him to the village doctor mush. I believe this was to Chilcompton a couple or so miles down the road—which they did. A pony and cart was hitched up, and the boy, who was too ill to walk, was carried out and put in the cart. All we could see was his face and did ever that boy look ill.

I must explain that most villages had a doctor living in them and had a surgery tagged onto his house—so it was to the doctor's house the boy was taken. It seemed a long wait, and when they returned, the boy was nowhere in sight and his parents crying fit to burst. It took long seconds to find out what had happened. They took him to hospital, they cried. "Where? What hospital?" Every one asked at the same time. The father told everyone that their boy had appendix or burst appendix and was in a very low state—now he was on his way to the big hospital in Bath. We got to pack up and get to that hospital.

"Did the doctor say it was St. Martins Hospital?"

"Yes," said the dad, "and we got to get there."

My dad put one of our horses in the trolly and told my mum to bring the wagon on. He would get the mother there well before the wagons could—so that's what they did, my dad and Rodie, and a couple of the other women galloped out the lane. He would trot or gallop most of the fifteen or sixteen miles to the hospital.

Jim hitched up our wagon for my mum and a long line of wagons pulled out the lane. The boy's father setting the pace as he was told to drive in front the others because they knew he would need a tracer to get up the two steep hills between us and Bath. This way less time would be wasted through Chilcompton and Radstock. At the bottom of the long hill leading to Peasdown St. John, the first tracer was put alongside the driving horse. Both horses would make short work of the hill and the dad could be on his way—at the top of the hill, the tracer horse was unhitched and rode back to its own wagon. Each wagon had its tracer, so soon everyone was on top the hill. The father of the boy by now had a good head start on the rest of us but a young man rode on to catch him up, for just outside the village of Peasdown was Dunkerton hill and the tracer would be needed to get the wagon up safely. On reaching the hospital, all the wagons were lined up on the road outside the hospital, leaving a group of older ones to keep us in check, every grown up rushed into the hospital—they were gone a good long while. On coming back, we learned the boy's appendix had burst. He was full of poison and it was a very little chance whether he made it or not. In those days, the medication and operations was nothing like it is today, and they never had the drugs as they do now. So it was touch and go for this young boy.

We were blocking the road so it was decided to shift the wagons on to a bit of waste-land half a mile from the hospital. No one would leave this family on their own—come hell or high water—and from here the women could take turns with the men to walk to the hospital. Always leaving most of the grownups to look after things where we had made camp, there were all the children and horses to be seen to.

This hospital, like all others, was very strict on visiting numbers. Only two visitors could enter the ward, the rest were told to wait outside but on speaking to a head person were allowed to stand in a wide corridor. It was a bad time all round.

At the camp we had several visits from the police telling us to move. 'Hard times' told them if we moved we would pull in on the hospital car park—which made them mad. It took hours to get one of the police to check with the hospital that we did indeed have a child in there very ill. They would not take our word for it but then said they would tolerate us but would keep a sharp eye on our doings—whatever that meant.

Then there were messages to be sent to the family members of the boy's family to let them know they were needed at the Bath Hospital. The messages were sent to different parts of the country and within days, our stopping place was crammed full with wagons of all makes, shapes and colours appeared each day. This kind of news travels fast as everyone wants to be at hand to help where they could.

This was our culture at its best. It was not just supporting the mum and dad who were at the hospital as much as the matron allowed. It was all the other travellers working as a team to look after the other children of Rodies family. Children were not allowed to visit back in these days—they would get upset and cry for their parents—hence they stuck close by each other and had to be coaxed to eat and to be washed. Then come bed time they would be washed and put to bed, where they would hug and cling to each other thinking they would not see their mum and dad again. So more crying could be heard from their wagon. It's hard to make young children who had never been parted from their parents understand, that given time they would come back. All young Gypsy children slept up in the wagons so they were with their parents night and day. It was sad to see their little faces watching the road, awaiting sight of their mum and dad, even with us bit older ones playing with them never took their minds off waiting and wanting their kin folk.

As so the women took turns in washing the children's clothes, another mother would cook for them; the men would look after the family horse as if it was their own.

As word spread, like it do in our community, relations of the family began to arrive, which helped the poor little children to no end. Especially when the granny and granddad pulled in, their little faces lit up for the first time in days. Now they had some one of their own. It was a huge relief to the other women in the way that the children were not going to pine so much, so that bit turned out well.

As far as the rest of us outsiders were concerned, we would not shift away until the child in the hospital got better or was buried. No one would dream of leaving them in their hour of need but we still had the law to contend with. They wanted us all gone, but no matter how many times they were told this could not be done because it was the way of the Gypsies to help one of our own in distress. They still could not understand our need to all congregate and told us so in no uncertain terms.

Looking back now, the big problem was a lack of education and understanding on both sides. All the police knew about us was we were a nomadic lot of families who chose to live this kind of life, who travelled the country-side. The hundreds of generations before us never counted, the police only considered what was happening in their daily lives. Thus, past generations were not given a second thought. We were groups who appeared and disappeared after a few days and that was it really. To make them understand that we did not just choose this life style, but were following in the footsteps of our ancestors was a waste of good breath. They just did not understand and never wanted to.

On the side of my lot in the forties or fifties, I don't think they would have known the right words or manner to explain properly what this part of our culture was all about. All they knew was they had to be close to the family in need and the hospital. To the law or local community, it looked from their point of view that we were being stubborn and wanted our own way and they wanted us gone, which we could not do. It was now a stand-off between us and the law.

The law had the back-up of the hospital, who had informed the police that the Gypsies were a nuisance by over-crowding the corridors, and making it difficult for staff to do their jobs, as well as the local residents and farmers. While we only had a tradition to put forward, in our defence, which never gave us much of a leg to stand on, which no one outside our group understood any way—or so we thought.

It turned out, that one of the local farmers did know a little of our culture. He and his father before him, had in times of need of workers, had let the odd Gypsy family stop on his farm, and so over the years had learned a lot about our way of life. So he had stood back over the past week or so and watched the goings on from both sides of the coin. He witnessed the frustration of the Gypsy group not being able to explain to the police, that this business now being discussed and argued over, was a major part of their way of life. As strong as the settled communities need of religion and ongoing to church every Sunday.

What he did next made him a very unpopular community member—in front of the police officers, he told a group of Gypsy men to follow him. He would show them a paddock he owned that they could all move on. Until things got sorted in the hospital and the young boy they could start pulling in the paddock today. Now everyone should have been happy, but not so the police, no they were not too happy with this situation but could not stop the farmer moving us to a secure and safe place to stop at. Luck once again came to our rescue from one kind and understanding man—from our women came many "God bless that mush."

As luck would have and God's blessing and the skill of the doctors and hospital staff, and not forgetting penicillin, the young boy made a slow but sure recovery. It was, his family said, a miracle–for they were told several times in the early days not to hold out much hope of his getting better. How happy we all were when his family said, "Our boy has been given back to us. We'er bringing him out the hospital in a couple of days."

But today things are very different for the Romani Gypsy Race. We now have a group called 'Gypsy and Traveller Law'. We also attend police group meetings on education of Gypsy needs, tradition, culture and customs.

We activists speak at these meetings. We also communicate with hospitals on every issue including food, visiting and tradition, and the need to congregate.

We speak in schools and universities to break down long-standing prejudiced views on our community, breaking barriers you might say, and the young students learn a great deal about our traditional lifestyle and pass the information on to others.

We enjoy working with these hospitals and police to get the understanding known of our traditional cultures and needs.

We have our own Gypsy and traveller planning agents to gain planning permission on private Gypsy/traveller owned land.

County councils have teams of Gypsy and traveller education workers who visit council owned sites and private sites to assist parents and children to a full education.

We have Gypsy and Traveller Liaison Officers working country-wide.

We work alongside the Racial Equality Groups.

We work with Local Authorities proving need for site and pitch provision of which we are in dire need of and in return the Authorities are glad of our knowledge on Tradition and Culture. It makes their jobs easier when dealing with a planning application for new private sites.

Many of us have broken with Tradition and wrote books on our way of life and given up a few secrets such as words from our Old Romani language which our forefathers would never have done or allowed us to. But books means knowledge and a way to learn of our traditional life style, a way to begin understanding our race or community, and I confess our Romani writings have been much sought after. They are very popular with the settled communities—as well as other Romanies who just love to read about the old days and old ways—a way of life lived in our past.

But back to the past, it was a very merry bunch of Gypsy families shaking hands and wishing each other well for the future. We had been in a dark place for long days. Now we were in the bright daylight knowing our little family had all helped and stayed close by, had a bright future too, so not one of us lot minded this parting because we all knew, God willing, we would all meet up again and yet one more episode in our lives to be put in our memory book of old tales; to be repeated round the old wood yog on a winter or summers evening, as all old tales live on, so will the most recent one.

Left on our own, all the rest of our company making their way to search for work, or going back to where ever they came from, left us feeling a little lonely. Now all wagons and horses were way out of sight and ear-shot, with their happy families most likely to be singing old songs because of the happy ending of a very worrying time. And they had a right to be happy and share with the world around them with their singing.

During our stay at Oddown, where the St Martin's hospital was my dad's family had visited most days, even bringing the old granddad with them on several occasions. So we knew he was, if not all that well, he was hearty enough and now we would make tracks for pastures new. Jim and Joe fancied a spell up round a favourite place, Devises, so it was now that lovely little Devises common we headed for. The common our little Emily, and Little Jess had been born on or brought to us by that bad old nurse on her push bike, hidden in her nurses bag hanging from the handle bar of her bike—as we young ones were then led to believe.

On reaching the town of Chippenham we pulled up in the main street while the women bought a bit of shopping and baccy for their men. Then on to the outskirts of the town to pull in for the rest of the day on the afternoon we set about making dozens of the pretty wax roses made out of all manner of colours of the stretchy crepe paper.

This was one job I and our Lilea enjoyed. It was women's work with no need of the men, so it was just us females grouped round the yog chatting and cutting up the paper. While our mums were cutting up the paper, I and Lilea were unravelling an old green jumper or gancey, as we called them, for its strands of wool to tie up the flowers with. While our mums made the flowers, after cutting up the strands of wool in to lengths, I and Lilea gathered the different bits of coloured paper in separate piles to make the dye for when the wooden flowers would be made come autumn; this we carefully packed in a tin to keep properly dry till needed.

Then a pan of candles was put on the yog to melt and get very hot, ready to dip the rose heads in and then the heads would be shook over the pan to get rid of any unwanted blobs of wax and laid out to dry. Lilea and I were never allowed anywhere near this part of making the pretty flowers, because we could get burnt badly if the hot candle wax got on us, and Cathy was laid up in the wagon to sleep while the flowers were being made. If not, we all knew she was unpredictable enough to get into trouble and get burnt, if she never fell asleep, it would be me or Lilea who would have to take her for a walk pretending to look for birds' nest, which she enjoyed doing.

Dozens and dozens of the flowers were made and waxed, tied on the branches of the ever-green privit and then ready to be hawked round the doors, which I and Lilea would be involved with as well. We two enjoyed our days out calling in fine weather.

These were long happy care-free days while the men took turns to stay back and look after the younger ones, we five sellers went out hawking, leaving Cathy with her dad.

Then to give the men a break, we would stay back while they went out dropping rag bills. Every one of us living in quiet harmony and enjoying each other. Life was just grand and dandy.

Then the day came, we pulled on to the little common—the birthplace of many Gypsy babies, including our Little Jess and our Emily. How well I remember the day the nurse called on our wagon—my mum had not got up that morning, so May, who we was travelling with now, fed us all our breakfast telling us my mum was ill with the old flu thing and was going to stop in bed a few days, which we never disbelieved, we never knew as my dad was gone to fetch the nurse who we learned in later years was a midwife.

On seeing this nurse in her blue uniform with the dreaded black bag hanging on the handle bar of her push bike, I and Lilea knew then something was up.

"O'doughty, our Maggie, that nurse got another baby in that bag; bet yer life on it."

"Well she ain't leaving it here," I told her. "We got enough of them babies. Bet she makes yer mum have it Lilea."

"Well she's up in your wagon not mine," answered Lilea

Sure enough the bloody nurse woman was getting up in our wagon, bag and all.

"Where's me dad at? He'll put a stop to her gallop," I shouted. "I want my dad."

"Well yis can't have him," said that Lilea.

"They's took the chavvies peg sticking member," they said we had to go an all—to help carry back the sticks and we never went.

"Well creep up to the wagon and hear what they's talking about Lilea."

"Shant. I shant me mum would hit me for listening."

"But she wouldn't hit you—so you sneak over there and have a kushti listen our Maggie, go on, and tell me what they's up to. I don't trust that nurse not one bit, I don't."

We never did get to listen for out came the nurse who jumped on the bike with the black bag and peddled off down the road. Then aunt May came out and told us two to fetch wood and water.

"What for?" We both wanted to know for we had a big heap of wood and all the water cans was full.

"I'll give yis two what for, get going and fetch that wood; do as yis is told for once. I said more wood now fetch more wood."

"O'doughty, our Lilea, we got enough wood to light ten yogs already and enough peg sticks to make enough pegs to last a year—our lots gone mad; they'll all get put away, just yis wait an see."

Well it was after every one was back we had a meal the two women had made. Then off went the men again—more peg sticks.

"Aunt Ally," I asked. "Why is the men fetching so many peg sticks? We got heaps of um—just you dick Aunt Ally—just dick at that heap of sticks and low and behold." afore she could answer me—there comes that nurse again. "What do that nurse want Aunt Ally—yis tell her to get back on that bike and git right away from us."

All I got was a pat on the head, just like you would pat a juckle (dog). I felt sick to me self and sat down by the yog—after a good long while a baby was crying and the crying come from our wagon; that bloody nurse had done it again. She been and talked me mam into having another crying, shitty baby and would be confined to bed to make sure that shitty crying baby lived.

"I give up our Lilea. I tells yis I gives up."

When everyone got back, they seemed pretty well happy while I sat and wouldn't speak to meself, let alone anyone else.

This experience was borne by hundreds of us young ones over many generations. Birth like a lot of other things was kept secret from younger chavvies.

I can honestly say—I did not know when my mum, or other women was about to be confined to bed as I grew up on the road. A lot to do with that is may be the clothes they wore back then but a coming baby was never talked about in front of children. And after getting married and having two chavvies of me own, I can't but wonder how the women of them days kept such a secret and then had a silent birth. For not on any of my brothers or sister Emily births did I hear as much as a peep out me mam or others that had been confined who we had travelled with. They must have been very brave strong minded women in them days. For a child to be born inside a wagon surrounded by other wagons and heaps of children, and not a sound come from the confinement wagon until a baby cried its first cry—it is just amazing. No I could never have carried that one out, culture or not, I'm not that brave. The gals back then had quite a few shocks when they grew up; I did I can tell you.

Yes this common brought back memories, as did most of our regular stopping places. Each stopping place had its own tale to tell and be remembered. It wasn't till I got married and looked back on my young life, that I realised what an amazing community I was born and bred in. What wonderful hard working people those families was. Yes, they had made part of their lives a secret but it was done to protect us and to give us a proper childhood—with no such worries as sex, or boyfriends or marriage. That was grown up stuff and was to be no part of a young childhood. Children could be just that—children back in them days and live the few years of childhood in peace of mind away from worries and cares.

Chapter 7
The Traveller Man's Trailer

It was a fine warm day and we chavvies was glad to jump down out the confines of the wagon. Had it been lanes we travelled along, we would have been allowed to walk behind the wagons but not on main roads such as the ones we just pulled off. But now we had full freedom, to hop and holler while we played—we spent several days out hawking the wax roses and, in turn, the men dropped the rag bills. We were doing quite well.

Then one day we got back to the common to find a snub-nosed lorry and trailer pulled in.

"It must be gorgies having a holiday," said May.

"But 'tis a kushti trailer they got."

"No my May," answered Ally. "Gorgies wouldn't pull anywhere near us lot and our men's chatting to them."

On reaching the group, we could see it was travellers well known to us. They had sold up their turn out and bought this little lot. It was now the late forties and it seemed things was on the change.

The woman showed us up in the trailer. Like the wagon, it had one room but with bunks to sit on either end, which the woman whose name I can't remember said could be turned into beds to sleep on. There was cupboards and a little cooker and the smallest iron stove I had seen. It was right pretty—you'll soon be getting one Lenard laughed at the man.

"I shant yis knows. My turn out is good enough for me brother." But all our men was took up with the lorry now. This they did admire, and the man was telling our men how quick he could travel from one part of the country to the other. While this was going on, our women was questioning the woman about the cooker.

"It goes on gas," she said, a bottle of gas stood at the side of the trailer.

"Ain't yis fret to death of that gas then," asked May.

"No tis as safe as houses my May," and on and on it went—question after question

Of course we had heard some of our lot had changed over to pickups and trailers, but this was the first traveller we had met who had one, and right proud of their new home they was.

But in between all the chat we was glad to hear me dad say, "I'll stick to me old horse and wagon my brother—it suits me down to the ground."

But we was all fascinated with the turnout belonging to these travellers—it was a new beginning—and nice to see, but we was happy with what we had. Our way of travelling would continue we thought, at that time, for many more years.

But a couple of years later, we had a tragedy in my own family that changed our way of life for ever. I have recorded the tragic death of our little brother, Little Jess, in *Our Forgotten Years* with pictures of his funeral.

But for now, we continued our traditional way of travelling the bye-ways and highways as we had been doing for hundreds of generations. It was our kind of life—a life we enjoyed because we knew no other. We were becoming the old fashioned Gypsies as more and more trailers took the place of the much loved horses and wagons.

We left the common at Devises at the end of the summer and once again travelled back to check on the old folks down the Prince lane. We had been away long enough. Once our duty was done by the old granny and granddad, off we would go again. It was decided not to go hop picking this year—the rag bills was earning our men a fair living and soon it would be time to make the wooden chrysanthemums and start thinking about the Christmas work. So once again on reaching the lane, we pulled up in front the pub at the top end of the lane. It was here cock eye Joe decided he would take a break and spend time with the old folks. Giving some of his other brothers the chance to travel which we was sure they would be glad of. The caring of our old people was very strict in every Romani family and is still so to this very day. Once they get to the age where they need help in their daily lives, the family will close in and take care of them just as they cared for us when we was young. This is a very strong tradition, which I hope will last forever. Only now in my twilight years do I appreciate this custom of ours and bless my two boys for being there for me.

Back on the road again, we headed for Bridgwater and would work our way round all the out laying villages and then on to Wellington. Then take a circle back round the Chard area. We travel many miles in a year repeating what other past generations had done, and you can bet your last penny, we took the self same route as they did. Our lives was one long repeat of our old departed families.

Shepton Mallet, Glastonbury Street, and then out on the old Swine's Jump road. Once again as we travelled through the dark wood of the Swine's jump, we asked me dad to tell us yet again the old tale of the swine that jumped to his freedom from the police or peelers as they were known. When they stopped on the road to give the horse pulling a heavy cart a rest. The cart so the tale goes held a murder mush being taken to Bridgwater to be tried for a brutal murder. We loved this old tale because it made us shiver in our shoes. This tale is very old and has been passed on down through our generations as I have passed it on to my sons—who I'm sure will carry on this tale for a few more generations to come.

Once on the outskirts of Bridgwater, we met a well-known young gypsy man, young Georgie Smith—no relation—but a grand flamboyant young man. His parents grew peas and beans so he was known to us. Georgie was a good looking lad who loved horses. It was rare to meet Georgie without him riding bare back on some fancy horse wearing a cowboy hat. He was obsessed with cowboys and trick riding, and he had a sister named Elderberry who lived to a ripe old age and passed away in 2017. On meeting him even on a wicked wet dull day, this young man would brighten up your day. He was a real character of the day and became a lifelong friend of me dad, and was with me when my dad passed away.

Georgie took up trick riding and over the years he became quite famous. He married and had a grand little family. His daughter Shaun and her husband are my close loyal friends today and Shaun inherited her father's love of horses so is keeping his memory alive by entering the show jumping world and doing well at it.

Georgie settled down with his family near Congresbury and became a well-known character in that area. Everyone knew him; his personality made it so he even became friends with The Kray twins who owned a garage on the Congresbury road. The tales they told him of their capers echo's round that area today. I should mention this grand man because he brought joy and happiness to so many people. I was a very sad person the day I went to his funeral and gave him a last farewell—R.I.P Georgie, we all miss you.

We met just about all kinds of people while out hawking—some grateful to have beautiful flowers delivered to their door and was more than ready and willing to buy a couple of bunches. Then there were those who shooed you off their doorsteps and, occasionally, the ones who set their dogs after you but it was all in a day's work. So I was always on me toes ready to run if needs be, but I did enjoy my days out calling the doors in the summer months but not so much in the winter when the bitter cold would do its best to cut your lips off. By going out with the grown women we young ones was being taught how to earn our living the traveller way and this do pay off, for like me mam who lost her mother when she was very young. It was left up to me mam, and her sister Ellen, at a tender age to go out hawking to help keep the family and the boys' early learning would enable them to become head of the family if his dad passed away.

In the early days, by learning us the old skills and earning a living saved many a family from the dreaded workhouse because our death rate back then was pretty high. What with the old T.B which seemed to claim many young married men to death in child birth and accidents out on the roads. My dad's brothers started passing away in their thirties and early forties from Cancer—or T.B in the case of Tom that is, they never seemed to have the chance to grow old in many families. Unlike today when we live many years longer in to our eighties or nineties.

Although we seem to have a longer life, the later years brought its problems—mental illness, drug problems and the taking of their own lives. Stress and depression. These things hardly touched us years ago. Most Gypsies, like myself, led a health free life, till old age crept in on us. It is a wakeup call as to how many funerals we attend in a year now. It's a very positive larger number than when we were travelling for different death reasons. Cancer is much more rampant now—T.B is not so much in evidence and child birth have got so safe with today's medical knowledge, it's pretty much unheard of in my community to lose a mother in childbirth.

On looking back, we had very few disabled babies born. As we travelled, we met at times hundreds of families like on the hop gardens or out on the pea fields, but it was rare to see a disabled grown up or child. I did talk this over with me mam in her late years and she confirmed my thoughts—she put it down too so much walking helped keep us healthy and the food we ate. Everything was fresh—the meat was cooked or roasted fresh. We drank and cooked with spring water whenever we could which was a great deal because our travelling pattern included the springs and most of all to a certain degree we were a band of free people our lives was our own. We lived and ate in the open all year round. We were a hardy breed back then.

As our learning starts at an early age, so does family ties. We bond tightly and that carries on through life. We may fall out and fall in but we still care and support each other throughout our lifetime. Hate is a bad thing as the old granny hated me mam but when shove comes to push it was me mam who looked out to her when she was on her death bed. Although the old woman had all her family around her, it was me mam the nurse learned how to wash and dress the wound that the groth had made in her side. It was so bad that none of her family could stick to do this job and the pain the old gal was in was awful to see, my mum told me in later years. The old granny should have been in hospital but she would not go and the family never wanted her to go. They wanted to be close at hand and by her side to give her a little comfort at her passing—no matter what had gone on between her and my mum over the years. Her own flesh and blood loved her dearly and this was their time to show her how much they did care and to give the outsiders who came to sit up with them a place away from the confines of a hospital ward. More of our traditional way of life, the funny part was, me mam said the old gal dragged on her two inch clay pipe till the bitter end and shouted at her off springs in the same old way as she always did.

But I well remember my dad coming back in the early morning of her death to tell me and that brother of mine.

"Yis got yer wish; is yis happy now?"

We too knew only too well the meaning of these words for hadn't we wished for years the old granny's pipe would flare up and burn her nose—and it did just before she passed away and another thing was, we older chavvies had lived with the hate and seen it first hand being handed out at me mam. But once she had died, we was never allowed to run her down for the bad times.

"Don't ever speak ill of the dead," we were warned and took that warning to heart and kept our thoughts to ourselves and here's me writing about me old granny's bad ways—sorry Mum.

Back to our time in the Bridgwater area—me and Lilea continued to go out hawking with me mam and May, and I must say we both got to be a dab hand at it. We could hawk like two little women and knew how to talk and respect the gorgie housewives—and better still how to talk them in to buying a bunch of our flowers or whatever we was selling at the time.

We met and stopped with other travellers on and off—and the main talk was these trailers. Our lot was changing their wagons for some was for it but a lot feared the change—they never liked changes to their travelling ways. So a few spokes got thrown in the wheels of this new coming era, you had to get a driving license to drive a motor on the roads. You had to buy petrol to run it—where our horses ate the free grass—you had to pay a motor tax and pay a motor insurance. In other words, you had to be a rich man to live like that, it was said over and over—no, no this would never catch on—there was also the real fear that some of our lot would forget who they were and where they came from. By living as they saw it—the gorgie ways—for it was the non-Romani that had had the first trailers and some of our older generation felt that a few of our lot was copying their way of life—not to be tolerated, they said.

But catch on it did for in about eighteen months or two years all me dads brothers would be driving motor lorries or pickup trucks—including me dad—and most by then would be living in trailers. It's in the fifties that saw the biggest change in our life style, the lovely bright painted wagons and carts and trollies was surely to god slowly disappearing off the roads and common lands, but all in all it never made that big a change. For the travellers still kept up their traditional work, they still travelled to the hop gardens in their motor and trailers. They still picked the peas and beans, did the swede topping, and could stay in one stopping place longer to drop the rag bills because they could travel many more miles in a day, to reach more villages, police willing that is.

So all the old ways like field work-hawking and scrap collecting still went on, the only change was we could travel to a job much faster and go to areas earlier unknown to us. Spreading our wings you might say, but our old stopping places was still a huge part of our lives and used just as afore may be a little more than before the motors took over.

Now the younger generation was becoming the new breed. Instead of buying a good kushti driving horse, they was buying a motorised one and dressing to match it, and looked quite posh as they did so. As changes happens in all walks of life it was now happening within ours. I often wonder what me great grandfather would have made of it all him being born and bred in a bender tent—as it happened in me granddads time he knew all about it—and now few chavvies couldn't brag they was born in a tent or wagon-but could say they had been born in a posh trailer. This is why I feel so privileged to have been born and bred and travelled the old roads, just as my forefathers had and privileged to have been born to my parents who lived by the old ways. And that my memory of them days is still as clear as a bell in me memory today.

Maybe I get the years mixed up but I can explain that mishap because we never lived by the hour or weeks or years. No we lived by the seasons, the years could come and go but it was the seasons that played the important part of our lives, and the work those seasons brought. Even now speaking to my generation if you ask when their children was born, the answer will be:

"Oh I had her in the tater picking season" or "I had him in the hop season or the pea picking season." It was the seasons that counted for us, not the years. It's like the mistake me mam and dad made of the time I was born, I was born in the pea field, and registered on the 15th of May but as time passed, me mam and dad was so sure I was born on St Swithins day on the fifteenth of July, as that's the date they gave me when I was grown up and asked so I would never dream of changing the date of my birthday. I keep to the fifteenth of July—a mistake on my parent's side may be but I just love their mistake. It tells me the kind of seasonal life they led back in 1941. It's all part of my personal little bit of history. Here I am, nigh on my seventy sixth birthday and can still smile and think of their date of birth mishap.

I may forget the right year things happened but happen they did. I know because I was there and lived it. The only year in the whole of my travelling days I will never forget is 1950, the month of May. 1950—that was the year the angels came and took one of the sweetest beautiful little seven-year boy ever to be born, back up to heaven with them. That was the year burned deep in mine, my two brothers, Mum and Dads memory—that was the time of that little brother of mine's tragic death—our Little Jess, which changed all our lives forever.

Moving on from horse drawn to motor towed trailers lost us one of our most beautiful part of travelling in the horse and wagon. Riding up in the back of a lorry, it seemed to us looking over fields and meadows that we were travelling at a hundred miles an hour, and just caught quick glimpse of the cows-sheep and wildlife—reached our destination in the blink of an eye. What we missed, me in particular and others like me, was the sight of the green hedges lingering in the shade of a big old Oaktree or Elm-that hung over the road to cool down ourselves and horses on a long hot summers day. As we plodded along— walking behind the wagon and stopping to pick a bunch of flowers or jump a gate in to an orchard and picking a pocket of apples—then running to catch up with the wagon again to take in and smell the banks of primroses-violets and other wild things growing in the hedgerow or banks. In the autumn, we could gather the slip shelled little hazel nuts that had dropped to the road, grab a handful of big black juicy blackberries and spot and surprise a family of fox cubs, or baby rabbits, or pheasants, being motorised we missed a great deal that had been a part of our lives forever. Sadly, now giving us a quick glimpse as we flashed on by, as I said before, I had a deep love affair with our free countryside nature—I longed to be able to bet the boys, our Alfie and Robert and little Jess as who would be first to spot or pick the first celandine of a new year or birds nest. We had great simple fun doing this. In fact, I got a clip round me ear on jumping down off the back of the lorry one day at the end of a journey on to the hop garden. It was the first and last time we had towed a trailer to sleep in while picking the hops. I would have been about twelve or thirteen at the time and we were living at Keels Hill, Peasdown St John but it was decided we would go and pick the hops from the back of the lorry on the long journey. I must have watched the hedges and ditches fly by, not giving me time to enjoy the sight of them, so had a mind full at what I had missed seeing and on pulling in the hop stopping field I swore in front of my parents—

"Bloody damnation dad. I wished I'd walked up here, we couldn't see anything. You were going too fast," then my ear was red and stinging from a hard slap off my mum for swearing—we were not allowed to swear, and they never knew what I was talking about any way. My thoughts were not their thoughts—I was only using words my dad was always using but they were swear words, and I paid the price much to our Alfie's delight—the little mush.

Oh we knew every swear word under the sun—but were not allowed to say them. I think my dad could make a saint blush or the devil cringe when he was upset, so could my mum for that matter, but not us lot.

But I did notice the things we had lost by getting a lorry, we still had our two horses but no wagon for them to pull. They were now pets and would breed a foal in and out—me and our Alfie would have long talks and agreed it was the worst days work my dad had done when he chopped our wagon away, bought a bit of ground and kept us there in one place, living in a big wooden hut that used to be a shop. It was purgatory to us older ones being stop still in one place. Travelling was in our blood and it never did cool down, we longed for that old open road, and I still do today, in this late stage of my life.

As far as I could see, the only advantage in my dad having a lorry was that he could earn a better living and travel faster—the brunt was not being on the road with our horses and wagons living the slow way of life. Seeing and sleeping in a different place every few days—sitting round an outside yog, eating our meals with smoke billowing round us, having fun fetching wood and water, feeling the rain on our faces or the snow pitching on our heads as we sat warm and cosy eating a meal round the fire, falling out the wagon on a spring morning to the smells of the countryside, and songs of the birds, now here we were stuck in one place. Getting used to living in a village—yes we made a few friends among the village kids but still liked our own company and just being together, talking away in our Romani language together. Although we fought like cat and dog, I and that brother of mine was very close. I and our Robert were close and loved each other, but the bond between me and that little mush, our Alfie, was more like twins would be. We kinda lived for each other, maybe it was because we were the eldest two—I just don't know.

So the travellers of this country got themselves motorised and were towing beautiful trailers about of all makes and sizes, living compared to the old life a fast more comfortable life style. The old travelling life was dying out, over the next few years it would almost be gone as more and more trailers replaced our wagons. There were a few die-hards still keeping our traditional life style up, but they are now few and far between.

Never again will the roads have dozens of families in horse and wagon heading for the seasonal work, never again will we pass a common and see all the different shapes and sizes of wagons and their families sitting round an outside fire with the wonderful smell of their cooking wafting down the road and the wild animals that once were used to us and would not be shy of coming close have gone back in to the wild.

And the Gypsy women and young gals dressed in their black pinnies, who come knocking on your door hawking their pegs and flowers. Once a familiar sight walking up your garden path, they too have sadly vanished, gone forever.

As I come to the closing stages of this my last book, I sit and relive my childhood. I can see the time we chavvies would each have a pocket of short pieces of wool and spend hours picking dozen after dozen of the sweet smelling primroses or cowslips and making poses surrounded by a few of their green leaves and bound with a piece of old knitting wool, ready for our mams to hawk out.

Picking bunches of the blue and heavy perfumed violets took more patience as the stalks was thin and short, but we did it on hands and knees crawling from one patch of flowers to another, till our baskets were full. This was dedicated slow-work, but so enjoyable. As we chatted and laughed, so did the hours pass. The kingcups was another matter—these beautiful golden headed flowers loved the marshy ground, but they were big flowers and soon filled a basket, but oh the muddy mess we could get into sloshing around in the wet mud to reach them, that's when the farmers trough became a bath or a nearby stream would come in very handy. Then there were the snowdrops—these little beauties loved growing among the brambles in the woods. By the time we had picked our fill, my dear little skinny legs would be ripped to pieces and bleeding from the brambles as well as me hands and face at times.

But the little wild daffie well just looking at the snowdrop and daffies gave me so much pleasure when I didn't know what pleasure was, all I knew was on the sight of them they made me very happy in me chest, I would get in trouble for just standing and taking a first sight of them, and being told to get picking they never had all day in which to pick which broke the spell I was in.

Watching my dad making pegs and how skilled he was at it but when he made the big headed chrysanthemum I was so enthralled. It was, I thought, his magic flowers to watch him take a length of Elder stick from a hedge and turn it in to such beauty was beyond me at times.

Then to watch him on the quiet with his horses they seemed to know every word he quietly told them, they would nudge him and sometimes they would lick his hands or his ears—they loved and trusted him in all ways as he did them. Many a time he's just been missed by the odd farmer when he had pooved his grys—in the farmers field late at night. I must add the farmers mowing grass field, only the best would do and just beat the farmer from catching him removing his mare's at peep of daylight. He could have ended up in jail but still took his chances for the welfare of his horses—so they could have a belly full of young sweet grass. This 'Pooveing the Gry' was done by most all travelling men country wide—it was common practice among the men.

But what I did not like was if my dad got into a fight. It always fret me, but not my mum as she knew he could handle himself, and he had big hands, much bigger than most men; he could hold his own and punch, it's said, like a horse kicking.

What I did like was them afternoons or evenings when we all sat round a kushti fire and the old tales were told, especially when stopping with several other families and the group sat round the fire was a big one. Oh the things that come out at these meetings, lots of sad things, lots of what I know now to be a glimpse of our history—things that had been passed down from the very old days and gossip. How they would sit and have a hearty laugh at some daft thing one had done—and as it got dark, their faces would be lit up by the flames and glow from the fire, great memories.

I just love now, to sit by me wood burner and let me mind drift back seeing my mum and dad as young people—seeing the old granny three sheets to the wind on leaving the jug a bottle of the Prince of Wales public house. She had filled herself up on milk stout and would fight the devil himself given the chance— her old black hat slipped to the front half covering her face, she did look formidable I can tell you and her singing was some like a foghorn on a ship. She was best left alone with the drink in her, as the old granddad would confirm.

The singing in the hop garden stays with me—how I loved and enjoyed that quiet singing of old songs, as it slowly began round one crib, till it was coming from all the cribs. Proving that everyone was happy at their work even if it was misty and cold, with boots and shoes clogged with the heavy mud of the garden, still they could render a good old fashioned song or two—like everything else, it's gone down in our history—may be never to be heard again. Then I think of some of the mystery's we have encountered over the years, ghostly things that cannot be explained.

One such old tale was told to me not so long ago—it concerned my Uncle Jim. When owning a lorry, he too had got in the new fashion. He had an old lorry and was driving two of his brothers-in-law back to Bristol—when all of a sudden, the lorry conked out and the engine just suddenly died on them. Of course, they never knew much about engines in those days and after poking here and there, under the bonnet—still no life come to the engine. So it was decided the two brother in laws would walk down the road looking for a garage—leaving Jim stood by the lorry which still had the bonnet up. The road was fairly straight so after going a goodly way chatting to each other, the brothers stopped and looked back to where they had left Jim and the lorry—sure enough, there was the lorry with the bonnet still up and Jim still stood by it, but with a mush poking about under the bonnet. Thinking Jim had got help, they turned back towards the lorry, not hurrying till they got up to Jim.

"Where's the mush gone," one asked

"What mush, I ain't seen no mush," answered Jim. The mush who had his head under that bonnet, he was told.

"You two are a pair of dinalows (fools)," he told them. "I'm a telling you, I ain't seen a living soul."

"But we both seen him with his head under that bonnet Jim."

"Knock me down if I ain't telling the truth."

"Try the lorry," said one of the in-laws. "Get in, Jim, and try the lorry."

"Yis pair of dinalows wants me to try a dead engine, but to satisfy you I will." On turning the key, the lorry fired up and they took off, all three feeling not a little shaky—so who was that mystery mush who mended their lorry? After that, Jim would not keep the lorry and promptly chopped it away. He feared it and never would have been happy keeping it, we are very superstitious about things that can't be explained. There were many such tales as this, and a lot of strange things can be seen on some of the old back lanes and roads, and not always in the dark, and a lot heard to there's a pretty little lane up in Wiltshire where we would have liked to stop in but the travellers who had stopped there, soon pulled out because a woman and child could be heard crying bitterly in the night time. Then there's a piece of road where the galloping of a horse can be heard and this is during the daylight hours. Many of our lot have repeated this mystery—all the mystery's that have been told round our fires could fill a book, a bit creepy but it's all been seen or heard by the Gypsy people of all ages down through the years with less wagons on the roads and more families getting more work by travelling by motors. Our wonderful old ancient cures and potions began to disappear—medicines and potions–the ingredients kept secret for hundreds of years, were now on the brink of disappearing—it took the handed down skill to make these old ancient medicines and animal potions—when collecting the herbs used to make these things, we were even in my childhood, warned if anyone from the settled community asked us what we were about when gathering certain plants we were to say just picking grass for the horses—that was excepted as we were always seen feeding our horses, these herbs were kept close to the chest and never revealed to the outsider. Generations ago, our men would cure the odd animal of a land owner who had been good to them, and it was passed on by the land owner to others; hence the Gypsy men became known to have a cure for most illnesses in farm animals and were sought out and paid to use their cures on sick cows and horses, and they, even my dad told us, when on this subject one day, had a cure for foot rot in sheep—God love him.

My dad told us to guard our knowledge of these old potions with our lives—as his dad and granddad had told him and his brothers, we asked my dad or our Alfie did if, it was our great granddad who had first made these medicines. Bugger mey no, he said—they been made by our lot since time began—so on thinking back now, I wonder if when our early Romanies first landed in different countries, did they bring these remedies with them? Then I think not, because would the countries they come from have the same plants and herbs growing in them—so there's a bit of a mystery here that may never get solved. All I know is the cough mixtures and chest rubs my mum and the other women made did work and I can certainly confirm the dye made from Elderberries worked and worked well. I just wish I could reveal all the different plants and herbs they used but I would be breaking some law or other. It's sad but today most of my generation has passed on and the recipes are forever buried with them, because I believe we were the last generation to make them. A few oldies like myself have made one or two but only for our own use, hence the end of an ancient health making skill and because of lack of education generations ago, nothing of these recipes got wrote down.

Yes the big change over from horses to lorries made a huge dent in a lot of our traditions and culture, you can't get back what is lost, so we have to learn to keep up with society, and a pretty kushti job we're making of it. There are not many of us left who remember all these old things. There is one thing for sure, this old gal will cling to our traditions, culture and customs till her last breath—I love my Romani roots and ways, and cock proud to be a Romani Gypsy woman. The closing stages of my travelling life began in 1950—with the tragic death of our Little Jess—it marked a big change for our travelling ways and a huge change in my mum, in a way we buried part of our mum with Little Jess. It was noticeable to us chavvies, the cuddles were gone, and that certain smile when we got them—don't think for one moment our little mum stopped loving and caring for us, she certainly did not—but she could not for many years show us the love she had before losing her beautiful son, her shadow, soulmate, her baby. My dad kept his pain of little Jess locked deep in his heart and soul all through the remainder of his life. One or the other of us would come up on him, having a quiet cry, but we kept stum as he would wish us to do. But my poor mum suffered no end, and I think she could not hold us close for a cuddle because of her loss and deep respect for that lost child, whom she could hold no longer. If I'm honest, we had known our Little Jess was so much different than the rest of us. Yes he would play with us. He would fetch wood and water with us—but his mum was his real life. We could never leave the wagon with him to do our little jobs without him either picking flowers or finding a pretty pebble or whatever to take back to his mum. Everything was for his mum. He was a pretty child with dark hair and lovely nearly black eyes and with the kindest personality. He never had a cruel bone in his body, loved all animals and still sucked his old dummy but not outside the wagon. He would whisper to my mum, "I'm going up to have a suck of my dummy."

He kept that bit private just him and his old dummy. I can picture the pair of them now—my mum sitting pealing taters or whatever and Little Jess sat close to her leaning on her lap, it was like she had an extra piece of body. I can still feel his little body as I cuddled him every night, because he slept under my mum and dad's bunk bed with me, Robert, and our Alfie. Where we would beg for tuppence or six pence to spend in a shop, he would make a hole in a wall or bank and hide his pennies away—most of our old stopping places still got his money hid in them to this day—and when he spoke he talked with a lisp—such an unusual child. Yes he was a little angel while on this earth—each of us loved him dearly and missed and longed for him when he was no longer with us, which gives us an idea what my mam went through for many a year after. That's not quite true it was for the rest of her life—my dad's suffering in silence—and the added big worry that they had had to borrow the fifty pound off cripple

Jessie to pay for the little funeral, which just had to be paid back as soon as possible.

For my mum's peace of mind, and it was round about twelve months later, we were stopping on Chaple Plaister when we lost this precious child, and because of her state of mind and health, she was four months pregnant which we chavvies never knew at the time, my dad decided to take her back to her sister, Ellen, down in Devonshire.

We ended up after several stopping places, pulling in an old stone quarry on the edge of Dartmoor, a place known as 'Ramshorn Down', it was here that my dad chopped away our wagon and I believe deep down, it was because my mum was turning it into a place where she could and did feel very close to her lost child. And so not making much progress with her loss— he had chopped out for an old radar detector trailer thing. It was not a pretty sight, in fact its wheels were so high under it, it looked like a cockerel on long legs, but after a big row on losing her wagon, aunt Ellen got her doing up the inside, by coaxing her along which took a bit of doing. My dad bought his first lorry, and he and Bob, Aunt Ellen's man, went out daily working together. I believe it was in 1951 or early in 1952 that we left Devonshire and came back up to Somerset—my dad had not settled down. In Devonshire, in 1952, we were pulled on a paddock in a beautiful little village by the name of Compton Dando. This is where we were invited by the villagers to watch the Queen's Coronation—my dad bought his first bit of ground for us to stop on. I've recorded this in *Our Forgotten Years* much more in detail. The ground was in Peasdown St John of all places, right near the Prince of Wales Lane and for us it was crunch time, our wagon days were over. It took a while for it to sink in that we were not going travelling anymore. My mum had made it plain she was stopping right here—and my dad could drive her back to the little grave up at Box, Bath where our Little Jess was buried—she had dug her heels in. And so it was right here we would stay, while my mum was quite happy to stay put–the rest of us were not so happy. After a few weeks in the school, with just me and our Robert, I had enough of being belittled, called dirty names and punched at almost every turn—had our Alfie been in the school most of this bullying would not have happened, but he never did go to school after an episode of schooling years earlier. As for our Robert, he loved school. He could soak up and remember most of what he was learning. As for the kids bullying him, it was a word and a blow; he sorted any boy that was nasty, but because he was younger, he was being taught on the ground floor while I was upstairs, and we couldn't even meet at play times. There was a place for girls, and a place for boys to play, so it was only on our way home that we caught up with each other. It was this school that turned me into a bully, I became a right spiteful little bitch—would fight the boys as well as the gals, even to the point of one father coming to our place and challenging my dad out. I had beat his boy pretty bad outside the school because he had beaten me in the school and because I had got the better of him, he told his dad our two boys had done it but after a bit of shouting, the father realised it was me, then gave him a clout for letting a gal beat him.

No matter what the teachers spotted when I was being bullied, they gave me no sympathy whatsoever and turned a blind eye, but over time it turned the other way. It was me who punished them, so I got left alone. But in my eyes there was no need for me to go through this alone, for down the Prince lane there were at least a dozen of my cousins belonging to my dad's brothers who could have been in school but their parents wouldn't put them in. They didn't need no schooling, they said so. That was it, at the place we called home, everything including cooking was done inside the hut. We cooked, washed and slept in this big four roomed hut but what we needed was an outside yog and there was plenty of room and places to have one. But we never did, if only we had a wagon stood on the ground it would have been something even our little rabbiting dog Bizzie looked fed up to the teeth, stopping in one place. If it hadn't been for my dad with his quiet warnings, I do believe I and our Alfie would have coursed big problems within our once tight unit—we two were like a pair of wild caged birds, and we also knew my dad was not happy. He tried so hard to hide it and made us two do the same.

"You must not," he said, "upset your mum. She's been through too much already." Meaning her loss.

We would never do anything to upset or hurt our mum—so tried to make the best of our road. On weekends, my dad would load us up and take us miles in the lorry. It was a family day out,

Weston Super Mare, Cheddar, and to the seaside at Weymouth. He did his best to keep us happy, and started to go out drinking more. If we had wings, we would have flown way over the countryside, but I and our Alfie only had our legs and legs can't fly. But underneath, we three were most unhappy; we longed for the open roads, the common lands, stopping with other travellers, mixing with youngsters of our own age and culture, riding a horse bare back—all the things we used to do. It's a pity, but I think I and our Alfie were at the wrong age when my dad bought that ground. If we had been like Robert and Emily and the baby Holly—maybe like them we could have settled better but we were not. One time, we made plans to run away and buy a wagon and travel together, for we knew the roads as good as my dad did, but no money in our pockets put an end to that plan.

We were just young children in our parents' eyes and had to do as we were told—and that's just what we did. My mum and dad took us pea picking and hop picking which we loved to do, it was a sort of travelling, but we always come back to Keels Hill at the end of a few weeks when the season ended—all the time we were slowly growing up. One day, we would be old enough to do our own thing, and that was the end of our way of life—a life we were born and bred to live. A fat lot of good the motorised change over did for us two, it lost us a chance to live out our life travelling in a horse and wagon as our forefathers and ancestors did. It was just our luck to be born too late or maybe just too early. What of the families who now lived in trailers—well, over the next few short years, they prospered, got on their feet you might say. They were working as hard as ever, may be even more. Second-hand trailers were being chopped in for new ones, bright shiny new ones and most now owned fairly new pickup trucks and were travelling many more miles all over the country meeting up with different breeds of travellers. We even heard that some of the groups had got into London—stopping on the old bomb sites, where dwelling houses once stood. With the new mode of travel, they were now spreading their wings and seeing places we never dreamed of seeing, the young married couples were following the parents in smart outfits. We were catching up with society, but still the gavers pestered them, moving the groups of trailer travellers on from county to county—local authorities were now building sites to put them on. Sometimes using old stopping places such as the old air drome at Weston Zoyland, Nr Bridgwater in Somerset, unused since the last war. They tarmacked over full cemetery's now unused and turned them into Gypsy sites, such as the one near Heathrow Airport—which is still in use to this day.

But the travelling families who did not want to stop on such places were buying up bits of land to use as a winter stopping place—this caught on and we had little private sites sprouting up all over the country—a little bit of God's earth they could call their own—where no one could move them on. Gone were the days when the men would seek out the winter farm work to get hay to provide for their animals and earn an honest wage.

Gone too were the families who picked the wild snowdrops and the little wild daffies—but not my family, we would travel by lorry now and pick our fill, right up to the sixties, and still go out hawking, but even this old job was slowly dying out—more money could be made dropping rag bills.

I really did miss picking these little wild flowers when it faded out, and felt sad that I would never again breath in that wonderful first sight in the woods each season—but positive changes had come on us and we too had to keep up with the times. One can't help of days gone by when we travelled on the roads and pull in near an ash tip. While my dad and Jim would be picking out the brass and copper and other metals, we young ones found toys to play with—then had to throw them back on moving on. Like the time we were passing the stretch of road where the hedge was a gooseberry hedge and I just could not pass up the chance of picking a bellyful, so intent on picking my goosgogs, I had let the wagon get a quarter of a mile up the road and had to run for dear life to catch it up before my dad missed me. These were happy days. And the fast flowing shallow streams and brooks in the hot summers, we spent hours playing in the water, while the men would lead their horses in to give them a good wash down—then chuck in a wagon wheel to soak and tighten up the spokes.

I also missed watching our mum's busy washing and boiling up their whites—hanging it all on a hedge to dry—picking the Elder flowers to dry and put among the clean dry washing to make it smell nice. Now at Keels Hill, she had a long clothes line with a prop to stick her washing up in the air.

I'm so glad I took the time to record all these little capers to let people know in the distant future how simple our lives were back then, even if it did change. I loved my way of life but never quite had my fill of it and neither did that brother of mine, our Alfie, life at the pace of a horse for us young ones who never had the worry of where the next shilling was coming from was a happy fantastic life. It was the grownups who worried about earning a living and where to travel and what direction to do it in, and looking back, what a grand job they did of it. I'm so very proud of my parents and all the other Romanies of those long ago times.

As the sites sprung up, more and more of our young ones got put to school—but lost weeks of their education by travelling with their parents to do the seasonal field work—of which they had no choice. Also the sites provided taps of running water and families could register with the doctor and get, in some cases much needed medication and in time got used to their winter stopping grounds, so in spring they would hitch up their trailers and fly like free birds to the area of their traditional work, which by the sixties was also under threat because big machines were replacing the Romani families who had worked on the land, for more generations than I wish to count.

Jobs so willingly carried out—like the weeks spent in the hop gardens, which were great if the weather was kind, but in a frosty and wet season, it could mean illness such as pneumonia in the older members, coughs and colds. It was a bad old time and job, because one could be soaked to the skin and stay soaked all day.

And sometimes if we got a breeze, the clothes would dry on you, then you would be in trouble health-wise—oh yes people sing about the great times out in the hop gardens but it could have its drawbacks—they forget the days when wet mud clogged their boots and shoes till it was hard work just to walk and clog up the wheels of the babies pram, till it took a man to pull it out the garden. Or on a bitter cold frosty morning when you had made up your mind that you would pick more than the day before to make the number of your bushels tally up higher in the farmers record book—only to find yourself so stiff with the cold, your hands won't work. Yes this did happen and more often than you think, when we would huddle round the fires that had been lit to fry up the breakfast and lose valuable time from the hop crib, these were the hidden drawbacks people never talked much about.

Yes it is great to hear about the old days and how we used to help and support each other, and this is perfectly true; we did do all the things like make collections to help some families in dire need and would share everything we had with each other. We did strictly live by our culture but our close-knit caring ways could upset others—for instance, our men were one hundred percent men, hard working men but along comes a police officer who thought he could abuse and belittle our men and not get answered back, they would not be human if on being told that you're a dirty thieving scum, that you have no rights because you're a Gypsy— and not answer back—and when they did, which surely they would, they would find themselves in handcuffs and took off to the local lock up–and once there got badly roughed up, and paid a fine the next day for the pleasure. I am not saying this happened every day, but often enough to stick in our memories. I'm not saying every police officer was tarred with the same brush but it did happen.

Then I have known our women to walk miles to a shop, only to be told we don't serve Gypsies in here. How belittling is that– our money was not good enough, and our families it seemed didn't need the food they intended to buy as much as the village folks did. What they could not see beyond their nose was, yes, we are Gypsies, we do seem to travel a great deal, which in fact we did but also we were a very hard working lot of travellers. We were the ones who provided their village butchers with fresh meat in the form of rabbits and such—we were the people who picked the peas, cut and topped swedes, picked up the hundreds of tons of potatoes, picked the sprouts and cut fields of cabbages for these people to eat. We were the workers who did all that—a fair day's work for a fair day's pay.

We lost countless young men and fathers in both World Wars, the very same as they did and our men fought alongside their men whose lives depended on trusting each other when in a tight spot, it worked on both sides.

Our children of the day, like myself, got served shipwreck in some of the schools and when we defended ourselves were duly punished for it. But what they did not realise, was that all the bad things that happened to members of my community only drew us closer together—that was a smallish reason that we most always travelled in groups—to help and support each other. We may have been dozens of breeds, but in times of trouble we became one breed.

So you see, it was not always the sweet romantic life our people were living, we lived by the rules of the land but also lived by our deep-rooted Romani tradition and rules.

We also did our own policing within our community—and the punishment could be very hard as a few found out over the years. One old tale that I did not understand when I was young, but heard bits of it discussed before being told to go and play. It concerned a man who had done something to a child—that much I heard. I was thinking he had beaten the child. I felt the punishment was harsh—this man had been thrown on to a fire, and badly burned—then made to leave the family, they disowned him. I did ask my mum about lots of things before she passed away. She lived with me for the last four years of her life, so we had plenty of time to talk—on bringing this subject up—she told me the man had assaulted a little child, this kind of thing she told me would never be tolerated in our community. And he was punished for what he done and banished from the Romani community forever and a day. Also she said, this was a dire warning to others of his kind—and this episode was cemented in the fireside tales and so handed down through the generations as a warning. We still do our own policing from within our community but nothing as harsh as our ancestors dished out.

I asked did it ever happen again.

She said that she had never in her lifetime heard of such a thing happening—if it had, she said they would surely hear of it; it would have gone round the country like wild fire.

So may be that Romani justice paid off, this man had broken our rules—and paid a very high price for it—had he repeated his crime, he would have met a fatal accident.

Other strict laid down rules are:
- We must never steal off each other. This was punished by having fingers broken, as a reminder not to steal.

- Never belittle our elders. Children or young people were beaten and chastised.
- Never not respect our elders. Again beaten and chastised.
- If a person or a family is in need, we help with money or whatever is needed. Lots of families back in the forties were quite poor still—some as the old saying goes 'Never had a pot to piss in' so a kindly hand-shake was often offered.
- We never leave any family alone to cope with death. We congregate round that family with help and support.
- We never burn elder or ivy; this brings bad luck.
- And where ever possible, we don't put our old folks into care; they are the family's responsibility.
- We never give a knife, we must receive a penny for it. Another bad luck thing.
- Never buy a brush or broom in the month of May, or wash blankets in the month of May; it would proceed a death in the family.

As I have stated, there are two animals we never mention by its name; it brings bad luck.

If a man or woman commits adultery, they are banished from the families, no one would travel with them. If it was a woman who did it, she would be shunned and distrusted by all the other women and would be known as a whore.

If a gal got in the family way, it would bring much shame on her family and she was made to marry the man responsible, if he was unmarried. If not, the poor baby would be known as a 'Bostaris' (bastard).

Our culture, customs and traditions must be abided by.

If any of these rules are broken, it can bring a punishment down on your head.

Chapter 8
My Mum

Every Romani child gets these rules drummed into them as they grow up—also our parents, in particular the dad, makes sure we are told. If you don't own it, it's not yours. The meaning of these words is don't pick up anything that belongs to someone else; it's not yours.

These rules was made so long ago, by our old ancestors, that we must respect them because back then the word 'GYPSY' was used as a rod to beat them with. If anything went wrong or was missing, the Gypsies did it. It was always blamed on the Gypsies, my dear old dad hated the word Gypsy, for he was of an age that he remembered all the things his dad and his grandfather had told him, reaching back to the 1800s, and my dad had the mind and memory of an elephant, so he never forgot what he had been told as a boy.

But it must be remembered, since the 14th century, we have been under the watchful eyes of Kings and Queens and any one like Magistrates, who was in authority, looked up on us with distrust and suspicion. Hence the Gypsy elders laid down their own set of strict rules—to keep our community on the straight and narrow path, and to save lives. This is not just folklore, our really old tales are full of rules and regulations. My mum, God bless her, was a great help to me before she died by telling me things of our Romani life that I did not know.

Some of the things I have recorded in this book about what happened when I was a child and also what went on, when she herself was a child and of what she had learned of our earlier way of life—it was only in the last couple of years of her life while living with me that she would talk of some of these old tales, such as the hard justice used back when her own dad was a child.

"Why do you think mum?" I asked. "Why did they not hand that bad man over to the law, instead of throwing on the yog?"

"I don't really know the answer to that," she said, "but it could have been our justice was harsher and would last longer—than if the law tried him in a court."

She went on to try to explain in her own way, that I must remember, "Many generations ago, we Gypsies had to sort of live like we were permanently in a shop window, on show. Our every move was watched with suspicion, so I think to myself," she said, "that if any of our lot had done really bad things back then, it was better for all, if they were punished by their own people, and outsiders were kept unaware of it what they didn't know, they couldn't talk about and pass it on—give us yet another bad name."

That made sense to me and my mum was eighty-five years old when she told me these things, so maybe, just maybe, she wanted me to know these things so that I could pass them on. If that is so, my mum, I'm doing just that, and I'm thanking you now for that insight of something I knew nothing about.

My mum was a wise little woman, who gave out sound advice, I once tried to tell her a bit of juicy gossip.

She said, "You know my Maggie, talk of people and talk with them, but don't talk about them. That, my gal, will get you in deep trouble one day." Yep, kushti sound advice.

My mum learned from a young age that life was not always kind or fair. She was only a child when she, her two sisters and her brother, Bobby, lost their mum. They had to enter a very different world than the one they knew. No longer did they have a mum to love and protect them because my mum could hardly remember her own mum. She must have been quite young when she had to with her elder sister Ellen, take a basket on her arm and go out hawking at her father's orders.

This, she told me she never minded—and did it for her dad, old Jimmy Small, willingly but this granddad of mine I learned was nothing like my other granddad old Dannal Butler of the Prince lane. No, this granddad was a man who owned little bits of land and who wanted more, and his children would more than help pay for it.

So he set them a task, he provided or paid for the swag they would hawk out round the doors and set a ten shilling a day return. They had to keep knocking on doors till they earned that ten bob—no mean feat back then, and to do it seven days a week. Then after walking many miles a day, with just a jug of begged tea to keep them going, they had to walk the miles back to where ever they were camped and start cooking the family meal and do the washing. Then get to bed in a bender tent on a bed of a straw-filled mattress, then up at 4 a.m. to start the breakfast then walk off hawking.

Their brother Bobby at twelve years of age was out doing a man's job, which he had to hand over his weekly wage to his dad and lucky if he got tuppence for himself.

This was not complained about—they would willingly work day and night to keep the family together. These four young children loved their dad very much and would work their fingers to the bone for him, just as long as they had each other, that's all what counted.

But come the day their father went missing, they were camped on a common miles from any dwelling houses—so it was a lonely old place to be—'Ring of the miyer' worried sick for their father's well-being. All day and night they walked the heather, covered common, thinking he had taken ill or whatever—then shortly after they spotted him coming across the common, he was not alone—he had brought them back a 'stepmother'. A very pretty blacked haired young woman called Annie.

But the four children were devastated because they had thought how well they were doing for their dad and promised to always look after him, but they had no say in the matter. He was his own man and wanted a wife so took one, and he had travelled all the way up to Bristol to get her. Life would never be the same again

It was not I'm sorry to say, the same ever again. Soon a new family was being born which added to the two gal's work. There were babies to be looked after as well as being out hawking all day—in all, seven more children were born in quick succession.

The family was at war. Bobby complaining about all the work his sisters had to do, was beaten and chucked on a fuzz bush and left home to join the circus and disappeared out their lives for a long time.

My mum told me that life without the protection of their brother got worse by the day. These are some of the things they had to do.

They had to get up at peep of daylight to go out on the fields picking baskets of mushrooms, walk off and sell them to the shops, then walk back to get their hawking baskets and go off trying to earn that ten bob for their father, still wearing damp clothes from picking the mushrooms. Another job was an awful one, they had to go to the oak trees and on hands and knees pick up baskets of acorns, so granddad could sell them to the local farmer as pig food. This job ripped their nails down to the quick as they picked or scrapped up the acorns off the hard road service—very painful

To think of the life I had led, my mum's tale had me in tears.

Neither of my granddad's first family got on with the stepmother but they loved their half brothers and sister dearly.

In particular, the step-mother picked on my mum's sister, Ellen. Ellen was not the kind of gal who would stick up for herself. She never liked to be the cause of trouble—my mum was made of firmer stuff and her and the step mother would have big battles, till it all came to a head one day when after being out hawking all day, the two gals got back to find no grub waiting for them—the step-mother had 'forgot' to save them any.

This time Ellen did say something—about her and my mum hawking seven days a week to put grub in the pots for her and her children. At this, Ellen was punched in the head by the stepmother who then sat down in front the bender tent. My mum was livid at the words used by the step-mum as she hit Ellen, she told her to 'fuck her dead mother'. That was too much for my mum, her dear dead mother had been thrown up—and her sister punched—so she picked up the kettle which was singing on the fire and threw it between her step mother's legs.

All hell broke loose, their dad screaming he would kill the two sisters while dragging his wife to the cart to take her to the doctor and the step mum screeching for all she was worth, in dreadful pain after being scalded in that tender place. She had the right to screech. It was an unwritten rule in the unhappy family that the gals never were to mention their real mum in front of their step mum; it would upset her—so the gals would talk secretly of their beloved mum. This was wrong and granddad's doing, he should never have made that rule, so when the step mum spoke in such a bad way of their mum, she must have had an inkling it would cause trouble and got it by the sound of it. There was no child welfare groups back then so no one to help these young people but one thing they did have were loyal relatives of their mum and their dad. My mum and Ellen walked miles to a relative, on being told what had happened—fed them and bid them bide the night, it would get sorted on the morrow. He promised, "Strike me dead if it don't."

Next morning, the relatives took the two gals back to their father—the step mum was in bandages and in a lot of pain, but both got asked why the two gals had run away.

It was all the gal's fault they were told.

No such thing, the relative told my mum's dad, it was no such thing—they two gals for years had been out hawking, cooking and washing, and not forgetting looking after the lot he said, pointing to the seven half brothers and sisters.

"Now enough is enough Jimmy. I'm warning you Jimmy Small, if you lay one hand on these gals after I'm gone, I'll come back and tie not only you but her as well," he said pointing to the step mum.

"I'll tie you to the tail of my hoss and drag the pair of you right through the fuzz bushes (gorse)—you know me Jimmy, I'm your cousin and a man of my word." After telling the gals to behave, he left.

"But," said my mum, "he, my dad, knew not to mess with his cousin—he meant every word he had said."

Peace prevailed on the common, neither gals spoke to the step mum—or much to their dad, which hurt them badly for they did dearly love their dad but they did start keeping back the odd sixpences from their hawking and the mushrooms and such. They, said my mum, meaning her and Ellen, had been unpaid skivvies for long enough—now they would start to feather their nests.

By this time, my mum told me her dad owned many bits of paddocks fields and an old garden nursery. The gals had done him proud—with their years of ten bob a day. Then a while later, he brought his family up to Somerset to pick the peas—that's when my mum met my dad and they ran away together near the end of the working season. On asking her what my dad was like as a young man, she nearly made me cry. She said, "I had him but never knew him."

This told me so much that she was unhappy at home, she took a man unknown to her and left her family—only to fall foul of her mother-in-law, the old granny. So my little mum never had what you call a good life. She was a good mother, but then had a great deal of practice by helping to bring up seven half brothers and sisters.

I know my dad loved my mum, but I think it was a long old time before she could say she loved him—at first who could blame her, the life he led her and the old granny made life very difficult for her, but she was a survivor and survived to outlive every one of my dad's family, including all sisters-in-law. She was the last one left standing of that generation, she also outlived my dad.

It was while she was spending her last years with me that I overheard her talking to a big picture I have hanging on the wall of my dad—so intent on telling him of the life he led her, she forgot I was in the room.

My dad had been dead quite a few years and I had pictures of him everywhere, like we do—this is what she was telling one such picture:

"Ah Lenard, you old bastard—you served me ship wreck years ago—I had a baby born with black eyes, because of you—I lived in fear of that old mother of yours and you, you long necked bastard never stuck up for me, but I did love you, you old bastard..."

I was in fits listening to her.

"Who's you talking to mum?" I asked her.

"Nobody, do you think I'm a dinalow," she said to me, getting a bit fiery.

"No, my mum, I just thought I heard you talking to someone."

"Well you never, it's the bloody telly."

"And what's the telly saying, Mum?"

"It said, I was a bloody fool for having your father," she said quite seriously.

I nearly fell off my chair.

"Oh dear, my mum, I'll switch the telly off if it's back chatting you," I said laughing.

122

"You can laugh my gal, but I loved my Lenard."

"You did, Mum, is that why he was buried like a colander with all the stab wounds you put in him?"

She never thought that quip very funny.

But it made my day to hear her firing at that old picture, some of the things she wished she had told him, while he was alive and living—she could be so funny at times, and would tell me.

"Maggie I've lost more sense than you'll ever have. I do believe that to be true."

My mum loved trailers so she enjoyed visiting the travellers that lived in them. My dad got her one, which they used for holidays.

Now by the late sixties and seventies, most of our lot lived in trailers with new makes coming off the line of the manufacturer's every week. So the choice was good, and much more posh than ever. They were by now making what we call living trailers—insulating them for winter use, making them longer and lighter to tow. I don't know a great deal about trailers, or the year a new one comes off the line, but my lot can look at an old trailer and age it in seconds.

The Vickkers, Westmorland Star, Bluebird, Hobby, Tabard Roma and Buccaneers, there is so many and I don't even know if I spell the names right—my mum and dad did—goes to show what I know about trailers.

Then the static trailers came into fashion—everyone wanted a big static to live in on their sites and keep the 'tourers' as a second home when they left their site to travel on their several times a year nomadic working times, earning a living in other parts of the country.

Years later came the mobile homes—talk about grand—these mobile homes where lovely; coal fire for heating, bedrooms and bathroom—proper family homes and sited on their own private sites.

And with each passing year, these mobiles was updated with the latest mod con in them—big bay windows, patio doors; you name it, they had it or should I say got it.

I now live in a mobile home. It's all of twenty years old, full central heating. It's a 'Manor Park' forty-six feet long and fourteen feet wide, it was top of the range when new, but the new ones of today put my little mobile to shame—seventy foot long and twenty foot wide—you would think it was a brick built bungalow from inside. They are beautiful.

Many non-Romanies live in these new mobile homes now—on what they term as 'park home parks', but this is a little different from ours. Ours is not just the standard made ones—ours is an ordered, custom-built one. The families get together with the manufacture and design the inside layout, and believe me, these homes are much desired and sought after.

When I am lucky enough to gain planning permission on a piece of land for a family, then revisit months later, it's a dream come true for the family. They have a beautiful home to live in, registered with a health centre, got full education for their children and fresh running water and a site they can leave at will to travel for work and have a place to return to.

And I do believe this all started years before with the change over from horses and wagons to motors and towing trailers—it took a very long time, but I think now we have caught up with society and are on the right track to have decent homes and get that education for future generations. And instead of sitting round an outside fire repeating old tales, our young ones of today can write theirs down, then we would, in the future, have a written record of our own.

Chapter 9
Kuwait

And so I'm coming to the end of this book which I have so enjoyed writing.

I have mentioned several times in this book, my first book, *Our Forgotten Years* printed and published by The Hertfordshire University Press. It was this book that put myself and a cousin, I never knew I had, belonging to my mum's real mother in touch with each other.

This is because in that book I wrote all I knew about my granny Minni Black, which was very little. It rang a bell with a person who read it that one of her friends could be related to me, so she made contact with her and related her thoughts.

And this gal did indeed contact me. Her name is Tracey Kirkby, who lives way off in Kuwait. I was stunned to find I had a cousin living in a far-off land. Tracey had my family tree, and it held everything me and my brother Robert wanted to know of our long-lost relatives. It was a lovely revelation, my first thoughts on reading my family were *aww mum if only you had lived a while longer* or *I had got that hand written book published back then*. I had it here sitting on a shelf while she still lived. I cried bitterly because this family tree had her real mum's family in it. It was such a fantastic information. One thing which would have pleased my mum was her mum's real name—Minni. It was a nickname; it was 'Sophia' which granddad had never told them—he did know of this because it was recorded on the marriage certificate, so he must have known. Had she known, she would have named one of her four gals Sophia after her own mum, but she died not knowing her mum's real name. Shame on you granddad. *Oh granddad, you old goat,* I thought. He of all people could have told those four mother-less children he knew her name and he knew all her family quite well. Why on earth would he not talk to them and tell them of their mum's family? You cannot blame the step-mum for this because he had ample time before his second marriage to sit them down and tell them they had a granny and granddad; cousins and aunties and uncles who loved them and would be there for them if they needed them. My God, did ever these four children need their relatives, they needed their love and support in their young lives. I have written in *Our Forgotten Years* how in 1951 some of these family members came down to Devonshire looking for Minni's children and found them. So they did care and cared very much. Oh granddad if you were here now, I would spit in your eye. What did you gain by your thoughtless actions? It doesn't ring right to me because granddad was so family-orientated. He would visit all his family in Devon all the time, make a big fuss of his cousins and others—so why not his wife's family? A wife who bore him six children, two died when young but they reared four—Ellen, me mum, Jeanie and Bobby, it doesn't make sense.

I was at a funeral back last year in Newton Abbot where he's buried. I sat on his gravestone asking him why he treated my mum, Ellen, Jeanie and Bobby, the way he did. Yes, I knew he could not answer me, but it was on my mind and he had to be quietly told a few things. When I think how much his four children loved and respected him, I felt sick.

But now I could talk to this long-lost cousin of mine. She was as excited as myself and said we were to meet. So she and her husband booked a flight and flew over. What a day that turned out to be. As they were about to land, our poor Robert had a heart attack and passed away, and he was so looking forward to meeting her and her family—that took the sun out the sky. It was not till the next day I slipped away to meet them—they had booked in a cottage at Watchet. We had spoken on the phone so she knew my bad news—I was in such a state, her husband who I call Charlie because I cannot pronounce his name right—he is Kuwait born and bred—had to come out and park my car for me. It was a sad meeting, tears all round, but oh how I felt when I hugged that gal—I'll never forget that meeting so full of joy but sadness at the same time for both of us. Her husband is a smashing chap and her son Mo is just adorable. It was a hard fortnight for all of us because my community did me proud by all the visits as we do by tradition and the sitting up at night. I had our Robert back to my place for his last night of sitting up, that way it included my new cousin's family, but next day when his funeral was about to start, I realised I had a blind drunk funeral undertaker on my hands. He could not see an eye through a needle and make no mistake, I had my eye on him because our Robert was a bit horsey in his later years, my niece was going to lead a beautiful black horse in front of the hearse till we reached the main road, and the drunk was to walk in front of the horse. He was nowhere in sight as we waited to start off. We found him in the hearse—I was sick with embarrassment and all the mourners waiting for my next move. What a show up, so I asked one of the undertakers to drag him out.

"And you tell him from me, if he's not out that car in a few seconds, I'll drag him out and chuck him in the ditch."

Well they got him out and stood him in front of the hearse with Cherry and her beautiful black pony in front of him. We got in the cars ready for off or so once again I thought—there was our poor Cherry trying to walk and lead her horse sedately and at the same time trying to keep Richard the drunk as a skunk undertaker in a straight line. But not him, he was rolling like a ball from one side of the lane to the other. One minuet he was up the horse's ass, the next in the hedge—he was turning the funeral into a comic strip—I vowed there and then to knock him down.

At last, he was helped back in the hearse. We arrived at the church. As we all lined up awaiting the men to take my poor brother out of the hearse, Richard came rolling over to me.

"Maggie I'm short of two poll bearers."

"What?" I asked.

"I'm short of two poll bearers."

"Richard," I told him, "after this funeral is over, I'm gonna skin you alive." Then I had to look around at my nephews to see who would match the other bearers and picked out our Ben and Danny and called them over to me.

"What's up, Aunt Maggie?"

"You two are going to help carry our Robert in the church, then up the cemetery." It was a lot to ask of two young men who had never done the likes before—God bless them, they never said they couldn't do it and went to the hearse. I felt really sorry for those two boys. I had thrown them in the deep end.

Now after a few wobbles, we were at last in the church. I'm seated and holding my own—talking and thinking in my mind about my dear departed brother—when again I got this misfit for a mush Richard in my face.

"Maggie, I thought, you better have these," pushing a bunch of the service sheets at me. With our dear Robert's face on the sheets looking up at me—I tried to rip the skin off his hand as I took them. This mush was driving me mad on a very sad day.

At the cemetery, some of the male mourners were going to stretch this Richard out—for there he was rolling like a drunken sailor while our Robert was being brought to the grave. I had my eyes on my two nephews; this was going to be the tricky part of the burial. I did not see Richard move down and stand on my husband's grave. If I had, I swear I would have ripped his head off. He was disrespecting my man, but the traveller women sorted him out and he came rolling in and out others' graves till he was standing over our Robert's grave as they were about to lower him into the ground. Then I heard the mourners drawing in their breath for this poor excuse of a human being was grabbed back from falling in the grave and pushed back.

After the service, which the kind vicar kindly let me share, this Richard was nowhere in sight. I looked in the funeral cars, all over the cemetery, no sign of him. Little did I know he had hidden in the cemetery's little chapel, taking his fill from a hip flask. The others knew but never told me till I got to the reception.

So on the following Saturday, I made it my business to drive to the undertakers as I knew he lived in the flat above the offices. So, I knocked loud and clear on his door and stood back—the door opened a crack, poking his head around the door he said, "Oh Maggie I thought you were the postman. You will have to come back on Monday, we're closed."

"But I am the postman and I got something for you Richard," I said shoving him back before he could close the door. Then shoved him in the office and pushed him not to gently in a chair—after a lecture which is unrepeatable to write it down—gave him some hefty slaps across his face and told him he would never ever do another Gypsy funeral, then left.

His partner came to see me and said he deserved all he got and would knock money off the funeral bill, which I refused. I paid it in full with money my brother had left, but vowed never to use their services again. One year later, Richard passed away—karma perhaps.

We had known this firm for over forty years. They had buried three previous members of my family.

But in all honesty, our Robert would have roared with laughter at his own funeral; he, unlike me, would have seen the funny side of it but I was left mortified. I've been to hundreds of funerals in my time but never one like this.

Tracey and her husband and son stayed with me for three weeks, and her husband Charlie took all of our Robert's funeral photos and put them on a disk for me.

I felt so sorry that on our very first meeting this beautiful little long-lost family had to land right into a bereavement, and never did get to meet our Robert, but stayed close to me and helped to support me through it—in fact, carried me through at times. The last week of their stay, we travelled around to the places of interest to us both. We visited old cemeteries up in the New Forest where the graves of my mum's relatives, whom I never knew, were buried. We scattered flower seeds which will flower for years to come, in memory of them all.

We visited a pub called 'The Fighting Cocks Inn' at Godshill where the inquest was held on a young Gypsy boy, who had died in a fistfight from an unlucky blow while fighting with another young Gypsy lad. It was fully reported in *The Western Gazette* in 1947, of which Tracey had a copy so we could read all the details of the fight. It was coursed by chats and tales which brought my mum's words flooding back to me.

Once she told me, "Maggie you can talk to people and talk of them, but don't talk about them." Sound advice, I think.

We had a drink in the pub, and it looked like it had not changed much over the years. It still had that bare old worldly feeling about it and we could feel the atmosphere of that long ago tragedy. The family was camped at this place called Godshill. Part of a sad report in the paper read,

'A poignant scene was witnessed after the inquest, when about twenty Gypsies were admitted to the outhouse at The Fighting Cocks Inn to view the body. The mother of the dead man collapsed on leaving the building, and had to be lifted into a waiting wagon, in which she was driven back to the encampment.'

Such a sad old tale and so much heartbreak for both families but it is all there recorded blow for blow in that old newspaper.

This was the area my mum's real family came from, they were the Hampshire Romanies.

We crammed so much into that last week we had together—they even celebrated my birthday with me—and when they left, she left a hole in my heart.

But it never ended there—during the last few days here Tracey was saying that she had never had a visitor to her home out in Kuwait.

"Oh," I said, "this is not right. It's culture to visit each other and you have never had a family member visit you my gal."

"No Maggie, not one family or other relatives."

"Well," I said, "I'll visit you and see your home and meet Charlie's family."

"Oh Maggie, we will pay your flight."

Flight, I thought, *means airplanes*—I never thought of that one.

"Yes," they said, "we will pay your flight and that of someone to keep you company and help you on the plane."

I had made myself a little woman by saying I would visit, our word is our bond—there was no going back. I was going to be flying on a plane—a plane of all things. *Why could it not be a train,* I was thinking. *A bloody airplane. How am I going to make myself get on an airplane? Never in this world,* I thought, *can I get on a plane.*

The two flight tickets came. It was booked six months ahead. Tracey and Charlie had to work out when Kuwait would be at its coolest for this big visit of mine. It's a very hot country.

Oh dear, tis true. It's really happening, but great, it's a long way off but you know how it is when you have a fear of something and I've always had a fear of planes and vowed years ago I would never cross water. There's a state I was in—my head and my heart told me I could do this thing but my mind kept contradicting them, telling me I couldn't.

And the months slipped by till it was time to go. I had taken Tracey's advice on what clothes to buy to wear in this strict country, but as I was in deep mourning, black she told me that I would be okay.

"But bring a sun hat," she ordered.

Me and the person who was going with me left by coach from Bristol and headed for Heathrow. The thoughts that went through my mind were driving me mad. *Perhaps the coach would break down and the plane would have taken off.* Did it? Hell, that bloody coach drove as sweet as a nut. I think what drove me on was that we Romanies never break our word, and I had given my word, so be it. Chest out, *get on the bloody plane Maggie,* I told myself a million times that day—I so needed a drag on a fag. I would have willingly given the driver a few quid to stop and let me have one.

On leaving the coach, the person with me had travelled lots of times so knew the ropes. Our cases were sent through and we booked in but had two hours to wait before boarding. We got outside where we could smoke, we both smoked—I was fairly eating my roll ups and shaking my guts out. *Who invented airplanes wants a punch on the nose,* I thought, *the villain.*

Now I'm in the departure lounge–we were booked business class, so food and drink was free and I could get at it.

"Please," I said, "get me some brandy." Which she did, because she could see I was on the edge of absconding—that went down well; my plastic cup was empty.

"Get me another please." By the time she was pulling me to the loading bay or whatever, I was walking rather high—my legs I could hardly feel—along a tunnel and an air hostess was showing me to a seat. This was it, I'm on a plane. I had been lugging a bag with a big piece of Royal Worcester, as a gift for Tracey and gifts for Charlie and Mo all day. The Worcester was very expensive and I was determined to keep it from getting broken, so I put it safely in a luggage thing above my head and breathed a sigh of relief.

Then along comes the air hostess carrying a hard case, and opened the cubby hole above my head where my bag was and was about to chuck this case in.

"Hang on," I shouted "don't throw that case in." Well the woman never let me get the next words out—she told me loud and clear I was not the only person able to use this.

"Whatever," she called it. Just because it was over my seat, and in went the case with a thud and started to walk away.

"Hang on misses," I called. "Come here to me a minute," and she did. "You shouted at me, and all I wanted to tell you was that I'm carrying a piece of expensive china in my bag, and I wanted you to place that case not throw it in—so if you have broken my china, I'll sue your drawers off you."

She got my bag down and checked it. Nothing was broken. She said sorry, I do understand how busy these people are, but she got right up my nose.

So I tried to settle in my seat. Some woman was throwing her arms about telling and showing every one the exit door if we crashed, and to put the seat belts on.

That's it, I'm getting off this plane right now, so I started getting my bits of things together.

"Where are you going, Maggie?" asked the person with me.

"I'm getting off the plane," I answered.

"Then you better look out this window," she said, "we're taking off,"

On looking out the little window, I saw the plane was shifting fast.

"Fat lot of good you are," I told her. "Why didn't you stop the driver?"

I'm stressed out now, my life ain't my own. I'm up in the air like a bloody seagull; trapped all because I had made myself a woman and given my word.

I've been in a few situations in my long life, but never one like this—six plus hours up in the sky and can't have a fag. I must have been the worst passenger ever to leave the ground. Here I am over seventy, stressed out, needing a fag in a seat with a blanket over my head flying about the sky. I should have had my head seen to then a tap on the shoulder—would I like a drink—champagne or juice. "Champagne please." I had two, then fell in and out of sleep.

No one will ever know how relieved I was to hear, "Put your seat belts on—we are landing."

Now I was looking out the window for the first time, I could see what I thought was a big town surrounded by a desert. It was a beautiful sight and more so because I was getting closer to it by the second. I have always been fascinated by sand deserts and here was a real life one; I was feeling tired but happy.

Then, on landing, I could not have listened too well to what my companion had told me to do on landing—suck a sweet or whatever—she said something to me and I had no hearing and no voice, or so I thought.

As she talked, all I could see was her mouth opening and shutting.

"I can't fucking hear you," I shouted, "I'm deaf and dumb."

Then she pointed to the people around me, who understanding English were in fits of laughter at this old gal, so I just hung my head and crawled off the plane. After leaving the tunnel bit, we had to walk a few yards in the open air and I nearly landed on my ass as the heat hit me—never in my life have I known heat like that and never will again, for this old bird ain't getting on any more airplanes thank you.

The airport was small compared to the Heathrow one, and a very nice gentleman was holding up a board with Maggie Smith-Bendell on it—he was to look after us and sort out our visas for us, and he got my luggage off the roundabout.

Then we was heading out to meet Charlie. *Meet Charlie,* I thought, *there must be a hundred or more of Charlies*, because every man was wearing the native Sheikh clothing. Long, brilliant white whatever, and the Sheikh headgear. Then I spotted him, and being me, forgot where I was; all I knew was that I had spotted Charlie.

"CHARLIE," I hollered in my glee on seeing him which brought all the other men's attention on me and Charlie. They must have thought I was a lunatic let loose, but oh was I pleased to see this man. He took us to his car and gave us both fags. Heaven, I had died and gone to heaven while dragging deep on the fag.

Then my first glimpse of Kuwait—it overwhelmed me. The houses made most of ours look like match boxes. They were not just big, but huge, with date palms in most gardens, mostly detached houses with flat roofs and very light colours. And the roads were wide and so clean. The whole place was so clean; no litter to be seen anywhere.

On asking how our Tracey was, Charlie told us that she was in hospital as she had fallen down some steps and broke a lot of bones in her foot, but he was fetching her home today. That was a blow to me—on reaching their home again, I could hardly take in the size of it. It was so overwhelming. On entering, two staff members were taking our bags and I, on looking around, realised I could fit my challet in one of their rooms without touching the sides. It was a massive three-story place—we were to spend ten days here being waited on hand over fist.

Charlie left us in the care of the two maids, who were brilliant. We had taken gifts over for them, of all manner of hair things, so they were over the moon with that—it pleased me to please them.

Poor Tracey came in, wheelchair bound, bandages up on her leg. I felt real pity for her. She had planned so much for us to see and do, but it made no matter, we were once again united.

Tis strange that when Tracey and her family came over here, they were met by a death in the family, and when I got over, there she was in hospital. It bothered me a little bit, such a coincidence happening on our first two meetings and two Gypsy women, strange, very strange. We Romanies picks up on these things, but I never mentioned my thoughts to Tracey, it would have put a damper on my visit.

As is one of our customs, we give gifts on first visits. I took over a figurine of Appleby Fair made by Royal Worcester, feeling very proud I had taken a bit of Gypsy china. Then they gave me their gifts, I nearly died on sight of it—it was a 1975 limited addition of a blue-face surrounded by diamonds ladies Rolex watch—worth thousands of pounds—and I gave her a few hundred pounds worth, it took the wind out of my sails. I was mortified.

"Shut up," I was told, "we love it."

I had not counted on the wealth of the country. It's a very rich country and the people there live so much different to us because of that—they have very different outlooks on life—and here is a cousin of mine living this life like she was born to it. And right back I believe to where we started from hundreds of years ago, near the border of Egypt; for I truly and strongly believe that we originated from Egypt, hundreds of years ago. When we arrived in Scotland and England, we were known as 'Little Egyptians', later corrupted to Gypsy.

They had planned, because of my belief, to take me to the border of Egypt, where I planned to get a little bag of sand to bring back and scatter on my family graves, but it was not possible with Tracey's leg problem. But they gave me a bag of sea shells to bring back instead. How is that for another coincidence—maybe that is why I fell in love with their country on that visit. It held some thing for me—everything delighted me, especially the gold market. Charlie took us to the gold market to choose gifts to bring back to our families. Gold is and always has been a Gypsy thing. We love our gold and wear it with pride, and here I find myself in one of the little gold shops with gold everywhere within reach. One only had to put out a hand to touch the gold and the designs of some of the pieces were mind boggling. And it was like a little street full of nothing but gold shops—everything to do with my long ago ancestors was ringing a bell.

I was so pleased I had stepped and walked in that land. If I was younger, I would surely go back—I would explore around that Egyptian border—I would get my fill of it—but alas I could not cope now with another flight. My age and health is now preventing that, but as sure as God made little green apples, I'm sure that Egypt is the land of my long ago forbearers.

We had another little surprise—Charlie, on my asking to take me to change my money into their money so I could get a bit of shopping done, refused point blank. It was their custom, he said, that they pay for whatever we want on a first visit. We were to take our money home with us—that never went down too well, I was so wanting to get in their shops. We did get in their shops, they took us on a shopping spree and footed the bills.

When Charlie's relatives came to meet me, they too came bearing gifts. The ones that could not come, sent me gifts—I was treated like a queen over there. They are lovely people and made us feel so welcome.

I enjoyed their beach, and, at times, we went out at night. The town was lit up beautifully. Mohammed, the son, took me out walking one evening. It was hot but much cooler than the days; the heat is so hot, their cars had to be started well before they were needed so that the air condition would cool the cars down. On wanting to sit out on the patio for a fag it would be for only ten minutes, with a sun hat and bottle of water. We were never allowed outside without that bottle of water, the heat could kill a visitor not used to it.

All too soon, it was time to get back on that dreaded plane—I kept my peace concerning it, but was getting stressed as it got closer. I so dreaded that flight home but could not stay any longer, our time was up and so our last meal and night came. The food was grand all throughout our stay. Tracey, over the years, had taught the maids some English cooking—we fared very well.

The flight home was in silence. The person who came out with me turned out to be not so nice. We were never friends after Tracey had arranged for a taxi from my village to pick us up. We had extra cases to bring home, so it would have been too much for me dragging big heavy cases to the coach stop. She had thought of everything.

It was a very tearful farewell. Faisal (Charlie), Mohammed and our Tracey. After take-off, I looked out the window and saw how high we were, I covered my head and prayed that I would get back safe and sound to my two beloved sons.

I think I come back a richer person in my mind. I had been where my ancestors had once roamed, walked on sand they may have trodden on, smelt the sea air as once they did. On landing and riding in the taxi, I realised how green our country was compared to Eastern countries—where it's far too hot to grow grass or trees. It made me realise how lucky we are in that sense. That visit to Kuwait will live with me forever; I so enjoyed sharing their home and so looking forward to their next visit over here.

Which makes me think how very lucky I was to have travelled and enjoyed a life that is no longer lived. How we got to know the old travelling routes—the villages some just pretty and some quaint—knowing in each village where there red phone box and red post boxes were standing. These were little landmarks we children looked out for as we passed through a village—the village shop, which held hundreds of wonderful things and the smell of its wooden counter where sugar was weighed out; and the cheese was cut to order by a thin wire, biscuits was delivered to shops in square tins, so had to be weighed out for the customer, paraffin and candles-cumalaters for the wireless set could also be bought. And the bacon was sliced on a slicing machine, and the looks on the faces of the shopkeeper when asked by our families to cut their bacon rashers on the thickest setting, looking more like belly pork than rashers, always brought a smile. Butter and lard was then in large blocks, so had to be cut and weighed—also salt—very little was packaged up back then. It was fun to shop, and gave you time to let your eyes take a dander round the shelves to look over the shop's goods.

When I think of our old stopping places, which was like a home for a few days at a time, and the beautiful commons which gave us a longer stay, and look at the sites of today which Gypsies own or rent off the local authorities, they cannot be compared—for comfort reasons.

The private sites of today hold just about everything, a permanent home from where the families travel off site and to come back to once their nomadic season is over. These are sites that contain a mobile home, a utility dayroom, fitted out with bath and showers and running water. Their yard is laid to golden chippings, beautiful gardens and play areas for their children and proper parking and turning areas, and a touring trailer for the nomadic travelling they do. These sites enhances the area they are situated in—we are very proud of them, and the site owners are even prouder.

What a different lifestyle my community now leads with their sites comes access to health care, full education and can now, with a permanent address, get on the voting register. So for the first time in most of our generations, us Romanies can vote and have a say. This is positive progress—I believe it all started with the change over from wagons to trailers back in the '50s and '60s.

Mind you, our Romani rules are as strong today as they were hundreds of years ago—our culture and customs are still abided by, by families on all private and authority sites.

As for the gaining of planning permission on private sites today—I leave that to my close friend, Dr Simon Ruston, MRTPI—Gypsy and Traveller Planning Consultant, who has his office in Bristol. He's a grand young man, who understands our difficulty in finding suitable land and Gypsy/traveller planning issues and problems, and above all, he has just the right personality to work with G/T families. I have known this young man for many years, and we have become fast friends and have worked well together and still continue to do so.

I am now retired from the planning for private sites—with health and age drawbacks—well past my sale by date—but I am still on the end of the phone to help or advise on any issues. I now spend a lot of my time in a small, mini museum I have on my site, educating young Gypsy children on their history, traditions, culture and customs and of the old skills once used to earn a living. The Somerset Gypsy/Traveller Education Team is involved in this, and the children love these visits to see for themselves how we once lived, to be able to see the old wagons and pots and pans, and most of everything we made back then to sell and earn our living is right here on display. It's hard for them to comprehend how it once was. BUT by having these groups of Romani children visit my site, it made me realise how little of our old Romani language they use, which makes me wonder if it's being used in their homes today. I don't think it can be, which is very sad. It is our old, closely-guarded language being lost among my community. Yes, I think it is—so to preserve some of it—I will write our most used words down here at the end of my book.

My working life is now at its ebb, but I have had over twenty years of planning and being an activist for my community—and working with other planning and activist groups, made many life-long friends. But one gentleman sticks in my memory and that man was LORD E AVEBURY, who worked for most of his lifetime on Gypsy planning issues and problems. Sadly, we lost this dear friend in 2016—there will never be such a man again—we lost our top advocate, he will be sadly missed by all.

Other groups that deserve a mention are:

The Gypsy and Traveller Advice Team—THE COMMUNITY LAW PARTNERSHIP, BIRMINGHAM. This group has worked tirelessly for the Gypsy/Traveller communities over many years and have helped a great many of our families. So, well done, CHRIS JOHNSON and your TEAM. I would take my cap off to you all, if I wore one.

And my good friends who have also given much of their lives by working so hard for our community are:

That grand lady, once a Gypsy Magistrate—Mrs Shay Clipson. Well done Shay, you have helped so many of not only our community but also the traveller community and have stood your ground involving racial abuse, and were never afraid to challenge the law on racial-hatred related crimes, and I'm proud of the work we did together. And to that wonderful Romani Gypsy lady, Rachel Frances, for bringing us together, we were like the three musketeers, all for one and one for all—I'm proud to be your friend.

Joe Jones, known as Canterbury Joe of The Gypsy Council—just to hear your name lights up my day. You have done so much planning on private sites, and worked hard on many other of our day-to-day problems. Well done you, my old friend.

Joe G Jones—who works with Canterbury Joe. These two men wrote a beautiful book together, after a visit to AUSCHWITZ, Poland, titled *A Road Trip to Nowhere*. I'm so pleased and proud of my copy, people who read this book will never forget the atrocities that took place inside these concentration camps, and the pictures in this book of inside this camp will stay in your memory. These cruel vile evil crimes must never be forgotten.

The Somerset County Council—Gypsy and Traveller Education Team. I cannot give this group the recognition they deserve for all the help and understanding they give to children and the sound advice they give to parents. Many children with learning difficulties would not get a fair chance at education if this team was not in existence. One of the team is Edwina Heard, a Romani Gypsy gal, who puts her heart and soul into her job and a close friend of mine, is loved by the children and parents she's involved with. Well done you Edwina, and I'm not saying this because you sold me your dear departed dad's twenty odd year old Roma Trailer. It is because you and your team mates have gained the trust of all the families you help—keep up that kushti work, it's much needed in our community and others.

Because I fear for my old traditional language, a language that was coveted and kept within our Romani community, a secret over many generations is now slipping in to our history through lack of use by our modern day lifestyle. The main reason for this, I believe, is to hide their identity from the local communities because it gives their children a better chance in education and of being accepted in that local community.

Negative press reports don't help matters, this I have found to be true by working closely with a Racial Equality Group—with G/T families suffering racial abuse and bullying of their school age children, this is more wide spread than you think.

Unlike when we travelled and were known and accepted as part of country life, where around our encampments we could speak to each other in more or less full Romani and no one really took any notice of this. The only real complaints we had while talking to each other in this way was when we got a visit from the law—they hated that we could converse with each other in their presence, without them knowing what we were talking about. It was really the only thing we had of our very own—our skills were used to make our living—everything we processed was on show for all to see.

That only left our age-old language, which was kept hidden and secret if possible, our precious handed down language.

ABRI	OUTSIDE
ACOI	LOOK or see
ALADGED	FEELING SHAME OR SHAMED
AMANDIE	ME
ALVIN	FOOD
ATTAPEN	PARDON ME or SORRY
ARAWNIE	LADY
ATRAISHED	AFRAID FRET OR FRIGHTEND
ATCH—ACTCHINTAN	STOP or STOPPING PLACE
KUSHTI BOK	GOOD LUCK
BALANSER	GOLD COINS, such as sovereigns
BARVALO	VERY RICH PERSON
BENG or BANG	NASTY PERSON
BISTERING MUSH	MAGISTRATE
BIKKIN	SELL or SOLD
BOUTY	WORK
BOSTARIS	BASTARD
BUDDICUR	SHOP

CURI	BUCKET
CAS	CHEESE
CHAROS	HEAVEN
CHAVVIE	CHILD or CHILDREN
CHIKLY	DIRTY
CHOKORS	SHOES; any footwear
CANNIE	CHICKEN
GAVVER MUSH	POLICEMAN
GURNNIE	COW
JUCKLE	DOG
JIN	TO KNOW SOME THING
JUBS	FLEASE
FAKE	GO—or FAKE ON—come on with me
JELL	same as above
VARDAL	WAGON
VONGER	MONEY
MUMPER	TRAMP
PANISH	HUNGRY
PIRO'S	FEET
POBBLE	APPLE
PUTCH	ASKING FOR SOME THING
ROKKER	SPEAKING OR TALK
SLANG	LICENCE
SHUSSIE	RABBIT
VARTIE/VARTING	SOME PERSON WATCHING YOU
STRALKS	SPUDS
DRIENGER	DOCTOR

I have recorded many Romani words in *OUR FORGOTTEN YEARS,* a book I am very proud of. We have hundreds of words in our language, some can mean different things—it's how they are used in a sentence—far too many for me to write down, and I do not know them all—as some like now have been lost over the generations.

To ever who reads this book, I say KUSHTI BOK and hope you enjoyed your trip down my memory lane.

Ann and Aunt Ellen's Roy at Ramshorn Down. Taken in 1952

The Bowers family at Binegar Fair in the late '40s

Uncle Bobby with the foal and Grandad Jim and Annie. Taken at Govers Hill in the 1950s

My husband Terry and my son Mike

Me mam and dad's last stopping place

Me with Prince Edward at a museum in Taunton

Georgie Smith out shooting shussies (rabbits)

Me uncle Georgie Smith's family pea-picking in the late '40s.

Theodore Griggs returning from Bridgwater pea picking to Frome

Me mum's aunt, Janey Black

My granny Minni Black's sister

My Terry and Jason in our yard

Me dad with Storm

My Terry sat on the kyt wagon

Me and Priscilla at a meeting in the House of Lords

Our Robert and me mam visiting relatives at Cricklade Wiltshire

Our Ann, Robert, me and our Olly at Keels Hill in 1953

Me dad's brother's (cockeyed Joe) wife, Ally

Uncle Bob painting his trailer at Ramshorn Down in the '50s

Me mam, Mo, Joyce and little Lenny in the '50s

Violet Small and Mert in Devon in the '50s

Cockeyed Joe, Ellen, me mam, Leal and me attending a funeral in the '60s

Me and Mert at Keels Hill in 1958

Georgie Smith at a western cowboy meeting in the '60s

32 Carlton Court,
Minehead,
Somerset TA 24 5PL
April 28th, 2009

Dear Mrs Smith Bedell,

I have just read your book about gypsy life with great pleasure. It re-inforced my memories of many gypsies whom I knew when I was the village policeman at Mark between 1948 and 1957.

During that time I became friendly with these people, and tried to help them with their various problems. I am enclosing a list of those gypsies who most readily come to mind. These include your Uncle Jesse – Crippled Jesse – and Young Jesse, your cousin, who later married Cissie Loveridge, whom I knew very well. Cissie was about your age, and she lived only a few hundred yards from my police station, with her adopting parents, Joe and Celia.

I'd be very interested to know who of those on my list survive. Most were older than I am, and I am now 88, but Cissie and Young Jesse might well still be about, as would Cissie Benham and her brother Sam, along with Tommy White's adopted daughter.

I was particularly friendly with Arthur Benham and Renee Hughes, his wife, and with Big Monty Hughes and his wife, and also with Andrew Bowers, his two sons, Henry and Joe, and with Alf Loveridge, who was younger than me.

I realise that you and the other gypsies felt that we policemen were constantly harassing you. Of course, I had to ensure that peace was kept in the area, and that the community was as happy as possible. Sometimes that meant having to ask camping gypsies to move on. However, I did try to give them as much time as possible, in order that they might have a rest, usually at least three days, and sometimes as long as three weeks, depending on the site of the camping place and the reason for stopping. Obviously if, for example, a woman was about to give birth, I would make allowances.

I would be very pleased if you felt able to contact me, as we clearly have many old friends in common. It is possible that I may even have met you if you ever camped in the Mark area with your family. Stories of gypsy ancestry have been passed down through my own family, and I believe there to be some truth in them.

So, thank you for your book, which has provoked such fascinating memories of many good friendships with gypsy families, even if at times we may have seemed like friendly foes!

Yours sincerely,

Tom Baillie

Thomas Baillie

Letter from a retired police officer who knew all me dad's family

Joe Loveridge, Celia (Hughes), Lena (Cissie) adopted
Jesse Smith (Bummer) – later married Cissie Loveridge
Crippled Jesse Smith, father of Bummer
Blacksmith Joe
(Dirty) Arthur Benham and Renee Hughes
Cissie and Sam Benham
Tom Smith, married Cissie Benham
Andrew Bowers and Diana Hughes. Andrew was the brother of Joe Loveridge
Henry Bowers, son of Andrew, above
Joe Bowers, younger son of Andrew
Diana(?) Cooper(?), Joe Bowers's wife, mother of twins
Alf Loveridge, younger brother of Joe and Andrew
Polly Loveridge, mother of Andrew, Joe, and Alf
Monty Hughes, wife Elizabeth Holland (?) and Elizabeth's sister
Tommy White/Frankham, wife Diana Hughes (?), and their adopted daughter
Walter Cooper
Caleb(?)
(?) Hughes, father of Celia and Renee, killed in road accident.
(?) King, carried an axe

Locations

Coles' Pea Fields, North Petherton
Emborough Ponds, camping site near Frome

There were two gypsy road accidents and two funerals in my time in Mark. I was present at one of the funerals.

Letter from a retired police officer who knew all me dad's family

Me mum with her grapes at Pedwell Hill

Me aunt Ellen outside her hut